M000313637

PRACTICAL PLAYWRITING

Practical Playwriting

by

David Copelin

Publishers The Writer, Inc. *Boston*

Copyright © 1998
by
David Copelin

The author is grateful for permission to quote from the following works:

The Art of Dining, copyright © 1978 by Tina Howe. Used by permission of Flora Roberts, Inc.

Doing the Book, by Stephen Reid. Reprinted by permission of the author.

for colored girls who have considered suicide / when the rainbow is enuf. Reprinted with the permission of Scribner, a Division of Simon and Schuster, from *for colored girls who have considered suicide / when the rainbow is enuf.* by Ntozake Shange. Copyright © 1975, 1976, 1977 by Ntozake Shange.

The Foreigner, copyright © 1985 by Larry Shue. Used by permission of the William Morris Agency.

A Question of Mercy, copyright © 1998 by David Rabe. Used by permission of The Joyce Ketay Agency.

Starker, by Todd Hammond. Reprinted by permission of the author.

Travesties, copyright © 1975 by Tom Stoppard. Used by permission of Grove/Atlantic.

Library of Congress Cataloging-in-Publication Data

Copelin, David.
    Practical playwriting / by David Copelin.
        p.   cm.
    Includes bibliographical references and index.
    ISBN 0-87116-185-0 (pbk. : alk. paper)
    1. Playwriting.   I. Title.
PN1661.C65   1998
808.2—dc21   98-36275
                                  CIP

Manufactured in Canada

Contents

for Diane
amor, comadre, compañera de mi vida

❖ Acknowledgments

I HAVE HAD A LOT OF HELP with this book, mostly from people who had no idea that they were contributing to its creation. If I've learned anything practical about playwriting, it's because of these people's knowledge of drama, their passion for theatre, and their willingness to share both.

The list of playwrights whose creations I admire is long. The list of playwrights whose work has taught me something useful about crafting a script is even longer. I shall not name names: It would take up too much space, and besides, you will create your own such lists. I believe strongly that every playwright, whether tyro or expert, needs to read (and see, as often as possible) the work of other playwrights, famous and little-known, living and dead, good, bad, and indifferent. The purpose is not to imitate their work, but to learn from it what you need in order to blaze your own trail as a playwright. A list of plays cited, along with publication information, is in the Appendix.

At the same time, not everything important about playwriting can be learned from plays alone. Four people—Marian Barnett, Robert Brustein, Gordon Davidson, and Michael Feingold—have shown me by precept and by example what theatre *is* and what theatre's *for*. My sense of the profession of playwright would be much impoverished without their diverse aesthetic visions. I thank them for their commitment, their insight, their wisdom and their comradeship. Michael, especially, has been a gift to me since college days. His penetrating comments on the glories and absurdities of the theatre, and his wonderful sense of humor, season his deep knowledge and deeper love of dramatic art.

I began to learn about plays in childhood, and this learning accelerated when some wonderful teachers, especially Helen Barr, Eric Bentley, Maurice Gibbons, Jan Kott, and A.M.

Nagler, increased my awareness of theatrical possibility. Speaking of wonderful teachers, if you ever get the chance to take playwriting workshops with Sam Shepard or Maria Irene Fornés, do so. I did, and both of them challenged me and made me work. They are both gifted, generous artists who teach without pontificating or prescribing how you "should" write a play.

Good actors reveal the spirit of the words, the heart behind the words, the links between the words, and the ineffable silence out of which the words are born. Actors whose stage performances have illuminated the plays I've seen them in include F. Murray Abraham, Stanley Anderson, Kathy Bates, Richard Bauer, Barbara Bryne, Jim Dale, Tyne Daly, Charles Denner, Jill Eikenberry, Laura Esterman, Edith Evans, Robin Gammell, Danny Glover, Louis Gossett Jr., Uta Hagen, Mark Hammer, Arthur Hill, Elizabeth Huddle, Holly Hughes, Bill Irwin, Glenda Jackson, Marcia Jean Kurtz, Ron Leibman, Vivien Leigh, John Malkovich, Zero Mostel, Ruth Nelson, Edward James Olmos, Peter Riegert, Madeleine Renaud, Margaret Rutherford, Leslie Sands, Ebbe Roe Smith, Meryl Streep, Kristen Thomson, R.H. Thomson, Lily Tomlin, Dianne Wiest, Georges Wilson, and Alfre Woodard.

I also want to thank those directors whose creative stagings of scripts both old and new have stimulated and enlarged my understanding of play structure: Bill Alexander, William Ball, Andrei Belgrader, Julian Beck, Steven Berkoff, Peter Brook, Judith Malina, Emily Mann, Jonathan Miller, Edward Parone, Lucian Pintilie, Ellis Rabb, Peter Mark Schifter, Alan Schneider, Oz Scott, Andrei Serban, Julie Taymor, Ali Taygun, Luis Valdez, John van Burek, Douglas C. Wager, and Garland Wright.

I owe Jeffrey Sweet many thanks for his friendship. He invited me to join Writers Bloc, his playwrights' group in New York; then he introduced me to the editors of *The Writer.* Without Jeff Sweet, this book would not exist. In addition, my former colleagues in ThroughLine (a playwrights' group in San Francisco), in the Marin Theatre Company Playwrights' Lab of Mill Valley, California, and in the Toronto Script Lab, have given me much good advice and moral support.

Brooks Barr, Margaretta D'Arcy, Mark Bly, Mame Hunt, Morgan Jenness, Marjorie Bradley Kellogg, James C. Nicola, Steven Robman, John Sullivan, and Zelda Fichandler have also influenced my thinking about plays and playmaking. Their mark is indelibly on these pages.

I owe special thanks to Sylvia K. Burack and Elizabeth Preston, my editors at The Writer, Inc., whose patience and support have been of great help. For twenty years, the late and legendary agent Helen Merrill provided me with good company, good counsel, and good gossip. I miss her.

David A. Coplin passed his deep affection for live theatre on to me, and Joan Blair's tales of touring with the Marx Brothers in the stage version of *Go West* still make me laugh. John Mayes taught me first to sing songs from Broadway musicals, then to value them, hits and flops alike. I owe them—my late father and mother, and my brother—an immense and happy debt.

Diane Marshall has believed unswervingly that I could and should and would write this book. My gratitude to her, my dear friend for many years and now my wife, is incalculable.

Finally, I thank our Eternal God for life, for love, for laughter, for the labyrinths of human nature, and for the unquenchable urge to write plays.

❖ A Personal Note

By the time I was eighteen years old, I had seen a number of musicals and a few light comedies on the living stage. I had also read and studied Shakespeare's *Julius Caesar, Romeo and Juliet,* and *Macbeth.* I loved the sweep and vigor of those texts, but I did not know them *theatrically,* and the differences between my suburban world and Shakespeare's dramatic universe seemed vast and unbridgeable. My knowledge of modern drama was derived from studying J. M. Barrie's *The Old Lady Shows Her Medals,* Rudolf Besier's *The Barretts of Wimpole Street,* and J. M. Synge's *Riders to the Sea* in my high school English classes. The first two texts are indifferent examples of twentieth-century playwriting, and they seemed so at the time. Perhaps we students were meant to conclude that, after Shakespeare, powerful drama was no longer possible. And yet, there was a bleak passion to Synge's play that suggested otherwise.

Then, in 1963, I saw Edward Albee's *Who's Afraid of Virginia Woolf?* on Broadway. Alan Schneider's production gave me the most affecting evening I had ever had in a theatre. My aunt, literary agent Laura Wilck, sniffed, "It's not a play." I replied, "Well, it'll do until one comes along!" Aunt Laura meant that despite the play's emotional fierceness, Albee's characters remained in their enmeshed isolation, not changed, improved, or even much enlightened. Her idea of what *is* a play is common enough, but I believe it's far too narrow.

I remember that evening as the first time I was convinced *viscerally* that drama could matter, that it could present an audience with a harrowing vision of a deeply wounded relationship that sustained itself with liberal doses of humor, endurance, and the battle between consciousness and denial. There was even some hope (however bleak), with what then seemed to me minimal sentimentality. For me, drama as

❖ What This Book Is For

THE PURPOSE OF *Practical Playwriting* is to get you to stop reading books (including this one) on how to write plays and to start writing plays. You can't learn playwriting from a book. You can learn to write plays by writing plays, or rather (as you will discover) by *re*writing plays.

Why this book, then? Because the impulse to write for the theatre, for live human performance, is easy to frustrate, to divert, to stop in its tracks. Even though there is no training for a playwright like on-the-job training, there are ways to keep the impulse to write a play from dissipating, from falling apart because you don't know how to connect that impulse to the action that will turn it into the reality of a "finished" script.

Practical Playwriting is an attempt to encourage your impulse to write, to offer you some suggestions and shortcuts that you can use no matter what genre of play you want to create, no matter what kind of theatre you're writing for. I am less interested in the particular writing choices you make than I am in helping you recognize and use the tools of your imagination, your knowledge, your memory, and your artistic vision.

Playwriting is an art. This art is created through expertise in a craft that, despite the wide variety of dramatic forms and styles available to you, has certain common principles. I'm not going to dictate to you what these principles are, because to overemphasize the "rules" of playwriting might encourage you to oversim-

1

plify the contrapuntal richness and complexity of really effective writing for the theatre. In other words, if there are rules to writing plays, you don't need to learn them as formulae that you *must* follow.

Never mind the rules, then; focus instead on the impulse that got you to pick up this book in the first place—the desire to write a play. In the long run, this is the most practical and effective approach.

In most plays, actors represent imaginary characters in a situation that forces one or more of the characters to overcome some challenge or set of challenges to reach desired results. When this representation is shared with a live audience, *theatre* happens. It's an ancient ritual, the most primitive yet most sophisticated art form yet invented. Plays illustrate, celebrate, and comment on human potential, human frailty, and the limits of the human imagination. At their best, plays— whether important or trivial—are sublime in their ability to make us believe that we are witnessing something wonderful, sharing experiences without which our lives would be impoverished, our humanity diminished.

I hope you will use this book as a provocation, a brief introduction to some practical approaches to writing plays. Read it, take what you find helpful, then get on with your own work.

❖❖ 1

Getting Started

WHAT'S THE FIRST STEP in writing a play?
      I would tell you, if I knew the One True Answer that the question implies. I don't. I've started writing plays in a number of different ways, depending on how the idea came to me and what the most striking image was, and I suspect that other playwrights do the same.

To test this suspicion, I consulted some colleagues who belong to ThroughLine, a playwrights' workshop in San Francisco that meets weekly to present, hear, and respond to dramatic works-in-progress. Its members have in common the drive to craft forceful, effective plays, and to learn what they can from each other. They differ in their writing methods, their visions, their obsessions, their styles, and how they begin their plays. Here is my recollection of that discussion:

DAVID
If you were going to advise a beginner on where he or she should start a play, what would you say?

JEFF
The two most common places to start writing are *character* and *situation*. Questions about situation quickly become questions about character: Who would be in a

particular situation? What would they do? How would the situation itself define the characters you'd find there? Or, you can start with specific characters or character types. If you start with types, you must sculpt them into unique characters by adding traits, or by chipping away at the type until you've revealed an individual within. I generally start with a specific character in mind: sometimes I see a total personality, sometimes just a single trait. You can also start with a *relationship,* such as a father and a daughter who want to communicate with each other, but who have great difficulty doing so. Here, the key idea is a relationship that doesn't work, and the play may move the characters toward a relationship that *does,* though on a different level from what either the characters or the audience expect. When you start a play from a relationship, your task is to show how the people in it are affected by events, whether they change or not.

ANTHONY
Whether they change or not? What do you mean? Somebody's *got* to change, or it's not dramatic.

BRAD
Maybe it's the *audience* who changes.

CARY
I'm prompted to start by something that I *have* to write about. I don't always know what it is when I start, but I have to find out. I don't start with character. I start with a situation. I ask, "What would happen if . . . ?" Then I try to find the action that makes what I'm writing a *play* rather than a short story or a novel. It's a plot question; the operative word is *happen.*

WENDY
I don't start with either plot or character. I go through a dream-like process of seeing images. There always seems to be a mask of some kind, an artifice, that I find inherently theatrical. When the picture is strong in my mind, dense and layered, I start to write. Now, this is only the way I *begin* a play; the inciting imagery has

to earn its place in the ultimate scheme of things. I'm interested in what the picture means in the continuum. Each event in the world of the play has to connect to something larger than itself.

LOREN

I've tried to start with character, but it just doesn't work for me. I also begin by asking, "What would happen if . . . ?" The question allows me to come up with different scenarios to explore, and it gives me focus and a starting point. I'd love to have strong images and strong characters right from the beginning, but they come naturally as the first question is answered. The story builds the characters.

BRAD

Well, I start with people and situations from my life, from things that I know. Then I build "What would happen if . . . ?" and more universal concerns into the action. I try to tell a story. How will the ball roll from what I know into what I don't know? That's the journey I set out on. And what starts out as real life gradually becomes fiction.

ANTHONY

I also start from real life, and from memories. Even when I imagine situations that I haven't been in, they need to feel real to me. They need an emotional similarity to situations that I *have* been in. Then the characters that I find there start to change. Play structure demands that characters change. Now, the images and feelings I start with don't always have action attached, but they lead to images and feelings that do.

DAVID

I'm curious about something. None of you has mentioned *theme*. What about that? Don't any of you start from a theme, or at least a premise?

JEFF

A play speaks as a play speaks: in events, not statements. The notion that you can capture the essence of a play by stating its theme—and that if you can't articulate that theme in a sentence, there's something wrong with the play—is mistaken. I've found that starting with a theme instead of an action can limit the potential of a play to a mere illustration of that theme. I'd rather create a complex set of human behaviors, out of which a theme—or several contrapuntal themes—will emerge organically.

Clearly, there is little consensus among playwrights on how to start a play—except that at some point, each of us asks, "What would happen if . . . ?" However, during the playwriting process, each element of a play—plot, character, dialogue, imagery, and theme—must get some attention from the author. That being so, it does not matter which of these elements you tackle first, because you will consider all the others, probably several times, before you're finished. *Wherever you choose to start is the right place.*

What should you write *about?*
Conventional wisdom says, "Write what you know." Seattle playwright-director Steven Dietz, whose work has been widely produced, recasts this as, "Write what you *want* to know." In other words, write what you imagine, incorporating only a minimum of what you already know consciously and logically, since it is likely that others know the same things in the same ways. Writing about these things is, therefore, merely recycling common perceptions instead of initiating bold and fascinating visions. While this can be comforting (and lucrative) in the theatre, it's of limited artistic interest.

Instead, use what you know to discover—and to dramatize—what you *don't* know. Write what you dream. Write, perhaps, what you most *fear to write,* whatever that may be.

This crucial choice is yours: utterly, wonderfully yours. What you want to write about will differ from play to play, for the obvious reason that once you've written a play, there is little purpose to writing the same play again—even if it was a big, fat hit. Your themes may persist, and your obsessions, but everything else—structure, style, character, and so on—can and ought to change.

Ultimately, no one can tell you what to write about, though many people will make suggestions. One of the great joys of writing plays is that you have the freedom to listen to all these notions without having to accept *or* reject them.

That said, this is as good a place as any to raise the issue of the *autobiographical* play. Common wisdom has it that every writer's first play is autobiographical, but that need not be the case. Anyway, whether a play that uses autobiographical material is your first play or your seventeenth is irrelevant. The real issue is, *how* are you making use of such material?

My first job in professional theatre was as Literary Manager for the Mark Taper Forum in Los Angeles, a regional playhouse that specializes in the production of new scripts. I read more than a thousand scripts during my time there, and I still marvel at the high percentage of playwrights who (perhaps heeding the "write what you know" bromide) submitted dramas about themselves and their families.

Such plays can be admirable. Everyone has a family (whether present or absent), so family dramas can easily tap into universal concerns with rather automatic credibility. Shakespeare's *Hamlet* is a family play, as is Sophocles' *Oedipus Rex,* as is Eugene O'Neill's *Long Day's Journey into Night.* Of course, most family plays attempt and achieve far less than those masterpieces do.

A great many of the new scripts I read were self-indulgent pieces about dysfunctional families with a perceptive yet misunderstood young artist at their center, shown as either passive victim, ruthless revenger, or some mixture of both.

Some of the scripts were comic; some were deadly serious; some were just deadly. Reading or seeing them, I often had the feeling that everything in them was *true*, that it had all happened more or less exactly the way the author told the story. And yet, *it didn't matter.* The plays were whiny and self-indulgent, and no amount of "It really happened just this way" could justify them. However factually accurate such a play may be, without *dramatic transformation* of the facts, a bad play results. The absence of this transformation in many autobiographical plays creates a paradox: Their truth comes off as rather dreary fiction.

The truth is that "truth" is not enough. It is through a playwright's artistic sensibility that facts are transformed, seen from an angle different from that of mere experience. Writing a straightforward autobiographical play may be therapeutic for its author, but unless it avoids the pitfalls of sticking to "what really happened," the play will not be much good to anyone else.

I am not suggesting that you *not* write a play about yourself and your loved (or hated) ones just because there are challenges involved. But if you do, you had better understand these challenges and work hard to *transcend the genre.*

How do you do this?

First, remember that you are not writing a documentary, and that no one could possibly find your personal story *in its raw state* as interesting as you do. Drama is a more objective art form than are novels or short stories, in the sense that a theatre audience cannot see feelings and motivations except indirectly, by close observation of onstage actions.

If you are telling the story of your family and yourself, there are some major pitfalls to avoid. The first is *a passive main character.* Many autobiographical plays feature a central personality who observes (sometimes with great clarity), who comments (often trenchantly), but who reacts to others rather than initiating action in her or his own right.

However, a passive main character isn't always bad, especially if your play *examines* that passivity and its consequences, as, for example, in Anton Chekhov's *Ivanov* and Tennessee Williams's *Cat on a Hot Tin Roof*. Of course, it takes great skill to make such characters effective. When an autobiographical central character is surrounded by more active, energetic, and interesting family members, the audience may end up sympathizing with the "wrong" people! If that's the effect you want, fine; but don't have it happen unconsciously.

The second major pitfall of autobiographical plays is *their tendency to become melodrama.* When the character who represents the author is portrayed as a misunderstood saint, and the surrounding family as villains, there won't be much dramatic tension. The playwright has essentially already told the audience how they *ought to* feel about the characters, and the (unintended) result is that they will probably feel nothing very deeply.

On the other hand, this tendency toward autobiographical melodrama can be extremely funny, if a playwright is gifted enough and objective enough to satirize his or her own self-absorption. New York playwright Nicky Silver is a good example. In Silver's early farce *Bridal Hunt,* Artie, a college student, returns home on the eve of his sister Lisa's wedding. Lisa soon reveals her secret: She is bright and ruthlessly manipulative, not at all the airhead she has always pretended to be for her father, her brother, and her fiancé. Artie and Lisa's parents, Abe and Selma, are quarreling because of Abe's affair with his secretary (who looks exactly like Selma). Things don't improve when Artie announces *his* secret: He's gay and has invited his leather-clad lover to the wedding. Abe and Selma go into immediate denial about Artie's sexuality, Selma has a quick affair with Artie's lover, and Lisa seduces Artie in an attempt to prove to him that he should include women on his wish list. Then things get complicated.

Artie is conceived as central to the play, but other characters are funnier and livelier than he is. This is a major structural defect in *Bridal Hunt,* and one that is common to plays that focus on autobiographical characters or stories. But even plays with such a flaw are not without value. Nicky Silver's comic verve and acute insight into cultural stereotypes in *Bridal Hunt* were so impressive that the play served its author well as a "calling card," alerting the theatre community to a raw but unusual talent.

Eventually, Howard Shalwitz, the artistic director of Woolly Mammoth, a small theatre in Washington, D.C., took a risk and produced one of Silver's later plays. It was a success, and since then, several of Nicky Silver's plays—*Fat Men in Skirts, Free Will and Wanton Lust, The Food Chain,* and others—have been produced internationally.

According to Silver, all copies of *Bridal Hunt* now seem to have disappeared, including his own original.

But even if an unknown playwright's first, flawed, autobiographical play is never staged, it may have real value in preparing the theatre community for later, more sophisticated work. Nicky Silver, whose first play was dismissed as "scatological" by some producers, is now a respected and successful playwright. The lesson here, of course, is to *keep writing*. It may take you time to find your audience, and for your audience to find you.

The third common pitfall of autobiographical plays is *their lack of a sense of the larger world*. The political, social, and cultural context in which a family operates will surely have some effect on the making of an artist (since that is often the subject of autobiographical plays), and yet that context is frequently ignored. Without dramatizing this aspect, a family play will almost certainly remain a small experience. Therefore, a playwright who recreates an autobiographical world needs to be conscious, on some level, of the larger forces that influence that world. Whether that consciousness appears directly as content or indirectly as resonance is your choice, but it does need to be there, because it's every playwright's task, in producer Zelda Fichandler's provocative phrase, to "bring life to life."

Theatrical autobiography, at its most effective, is more than just a telling of one's own story; it has the potential to go beyond its expected limitations and become a dramatic symbol of an entire nation, or generation, or class. Eugene O'Neill's *Long Day's Journey into Night* is a powerful example of a play that fulfills this demanding mandate. The Tyrone family, though clearly *based* on O'Neill's, has its own complex, resonant life. Somehow, the specifics of O'Neill's play become affecting generalities about family dynamics and the relationships between function and dysfunction.

In different ways, Tony Kushner's *Angels in America,* with its powerful interplay of public and private lives, its multiple levels of deception and clarification, of wounding and of healing, is another good example. Exhilarating, complex, and humane, *Angels in America* does not at first appear to be an autobiographical play, yet perhaps it can be seen as a play about the coming to maturity of the United States itself. Any playwright who wants to create an autobiographical drama that transcends the ordinary can learn a lot from the power and scope of *Angels in America,* as well as from its attention to the constant interaction of personality, character, and society.

How can *you* avoid the pitfalls of autobiographical playwriting?

Probably your best way to escape passivity and predictability in an autobiographical play is, first, *write your play from the point of view of someone other than yourself, perhaps the character you like the least.* That will give you the aesthetic and psychological distance from your own story that you need in order to keep some perspective, and a proper distribution of dramatic energy among the characters.

Second, *don't tie yourself too tightly to realism.*

Realism deals primarily with surfaces, with appearances, with things as we are used to seeing them. Yet who has not experienced the occasional feeling that his or her family is in fact *sur*real, that his or her close relatives are demons or vampires, that family life is a nightmare, that "family values" are excuses for psychic torture? Whether this is actually the case or not, you can try to use such perceptions in an imaginative way. Forget about justifying your life by showing the world how crass and insensitive your family is (or was), and how correspondingly sensitive you are. This may be true, but it's banal. Instead, dramatize your story in as fresh and original a way as possible.

Consider this, too: For the past century or so, most plays have been *realistic;* that is, their characters are more or less like the standard middle-class theatre audience, and the mirror they hold up to nature is pretty much like the one in your bathroom: The view may be agreeable or disagreeable, but there are few surprises. So, if most plays are realistic, and if most first plays are autobiographical, and if you are writing a realistic autobiographical play, you can see how difficult it must be to stand out in the crowd. Aesthetics aside, the best reason to avoid realism in your autobiographical play is that there's simply too much competition.

On the other hand, if realism is the way you see your play, then go ahead and write it that way, and damn the competition. Who knows? You may get beyond the ordinary limitations of such plays in ways no one but you can imagine. Realism has been pronounced dead many times, yet it refuses to die—very much like the theatre itself.

Something in your mind's eye is making you see a *play*—not a poem, not a novel, not a short story, not a movie, not a sermon, but a *play*. Take this fact as a sign, let its energy flow from your brain onto your keyboard, and get cracking.

You can start with the world as you experience it, right on the surface. Like other writers of fiction, playwrights often find ideas for their plays in the newspaper. News that appears to be commonplace may have a hidden dramatic dimension. A perceptive writer may combine his or her insight into the seemingly mundane with playcrafting skill, thereby transforming the *ordinary* into a resonant *dramatic* event.

You can also start with something bizarre. The most unlikely tale can make a play, if it has magnetism, forward motion, and something important at stake: *The audience wants to see how it comes out. The National Enquirer* and similar tabloids are full of weird stories. They may or may not be literally true, but many are extremely provocative. Try to find one that appeals to your sense of theatrical possibility, that gets your imagination going.

Dreams, daydreams, hallucinations—all are fertile sources for beginning a play. Some writers keep "image bank" journals, writing down arresting, detailed scenes they observe or imagine. If a particular image or series of images retains its potency for you over time, explore it dramatically. Populate it. Set it in motion.

But aren't *words* the playwright's primary tool?

While words are certainly the primary *result* of a playwright's labors, at least on paper, some dramatists use *actors* as their primary creative tool. They may write a role for a particular actor, or they may introduce an object or a theme around which a company of actors improvises. Lines generated spontaneously, deriving from action, can then be distilled into drama. Such a process may appear to be disorganized and unpredictable, but in the right hands, it can produce stunning results. British playwright Caryl Churchill has used this method in her work with the Joint Stock Company to create such plays as *Top Girls, Fen* and *Cloud 9.* Ultimately, Churchill's words are as impressive as those of most playwrights who work more conventionally; she just discovers them by an unusual yet viable route.

And then there's music. Music is such an effective shortcut to evoking emotion that playwrights have been known to start new scripts by listening to music, then using the feelings raised thereby to help them create character, setting, atmosphere, and even the rhythm of the dialogue. In their stage directions, many playwrights are quite specific about the use of music in their plays. With music, especially with the music you listened to as you wrote the lines, you can recreate the emotional subtext of your play each time it is performed. The production brings out the audience's emotions and associated memories, setting them up for guided response to the tale you are presenting—with *you* as the guide.

Let's say you already have your story and characters clearly in mind. Where, then, should you start to write the story? From the beginning? In the middle? Near the end? With the scene that excites you most?

The answer to all such questions is "Yes."

Ultimately, there are *no* hard-and-fast rules about where you "should" begin a play. Where and how to begin a play is a personal, as well as an artistic, choice with artistic consequences. No doubt you can start a play in a place that may prove not to be as successful as starting somewhere else, but you may need to make that false start in order to recognize the true one later on. Two different playwrights treating the same subject will almost certainly start their plays in completely different places. Is there a way to predict which play will be more theatrically persuasive, more artistically successful? There is not.

Just *start,* and *keep going*. That's the real rule. Wherever you start your play, you'll take a fabulous journey, full of wrong but fascinating turnings, spiced by moments of inspiration that actually may help you solve problems in your script that had seemed unsolvable.

You'll write, you'll rewrite, you'll restructure, and you'll cut. Cutting bad writing is easy. Learning to cut or transpose *good* writing that is misplaced, repetitive, or that does not move your play on to its dramatic climax and satisfying conclusion is much harder.

As you move from draft to draft, elements will alter when you least expect them to. Characters may assume new attributes, change gender, race, or social class, or they may disappear entirely. Story lines will go awry—sometimes in very exciting ways. It all depends on where your imagination, your instincts, and your hard work lead you. Whether your particular talent is for acute observation of the world, or for a strong imaginative interpretation of it, you will be creating a new dramatic universe, a theatrical *idea*.

No one else could possibly do that quite the way you can.

That's why the best place to start writing your play is . . . *now*.

❖❖ 2

Characters with Character

WHICH IS MORE IMPORTANT TO A PLAY: character or plot?

In the creation of a play, plot is as crucial to character development as character is to plot development. We speak of *plot* and *character* as if they were separate entities with clearly defined boundaries, but that is merely for analytical convenience. For most playwrights, at every stage of the writing process, plot and character are intertwined, symbiotic, inseparable—yet you may find it useful to focus on plot and character as if each were autonomous, independent of the other. Let's start with character—not because it's more important than plot, but because characters are what modern audiences tend to remember most clearly about the plays they see.

One of the greatest rewards of writing for the stage lies in creating memorable characters. And one of the first questions prospective producers ask is, "How many characters does the play have?"

This question has little to do with artistic values, and a lot to do with economics. It has influenced playwriting for years, for both good and ill. The stark fact is that plays with only a few characters stand a better chance of production than plays with larger casts, simply because they are less expensive to put on and therefore are potentially more lucrative for the producers. Does this mean that you should restrict yourself to small-cast plays, even when doing so might make the difference between success and failure?

The answer here really depends on what kind of artistic vision you want to dramatize. Some plays have large casts because the playwright wants to put a complete and particular world on stage, with all its variety and complexity. But only a few producers can afford large-cast plays. These days, musicals tend to have larger casts than straight plays, because spectacle is so much a part of the musical theatre experience, and because higher prices can be charged for the tickets.

So should you voluntarily write only "small" plays? There are two schools of thought on this. One would say, "Yes, write for the market that exists, especially if you are a relatively unknown playwright." The other school would be more likely to urge you to pursue your vision, to write the play that you *need* to write, and let it find its own market—or create a new one.

This choice is entirely up to you—and what you see as the demands of your play.

Some plays *need* a large canvas. There is a good deal of aesthetic pleasure to be derived from a full stage with brilliantly choreographed crowd scenes. Other dramatic experiences, however, focus effectively on two or three people, with no sense of artistic compromise involved. The most sensible approach is probably to write small-cast plays first, get produced, become known as a good playwright, then look for a theatre that specializes in new, large-cast dramas and persuade them to commission you to write bigger plays, if that's where your talent is taking you.

But your task, at this point, is not to try to outfox the play market; it is to write a play with fascinating characters and a strong plot. The most intriguing moment in the playwriting process occurs when characters you have invented start to develop traits you never imagined for them, changing in ways that make them seem almost autonomous, creating *themselves*. That's a cliché, but it really does happen.

Although such moments can't be guaranteed, you can prepare for them. Let's look at three aspects of creating character:

1. The *verbal*

To dramatize the world is to unmask it. A novelist can describe characters at length, telling who they are, what they look like, what they think and feel, and even how readers should react to them, but a playwright's characters must unmask *themselves,* and quickly. Characters reveal who they are through their behavior on stage: their words, whether in soliloquy, aside, or dialogue; their interaction with other characters; their strategic silences; their presence or absence in a particular scene. Stage characters also comment on and to each other.

Since plays are compressed in time and space, a little has to stand for a lot. So, to the extent that you can sketch a character's "character" with a few lines of dialogue, or through a minimal number of gestures, you will master dramatic economy. In good plays, such economy reveals both character and the world surrounding that character in theatrical ways that involve an audience emotionally and intellectually.

Depending on who they are and what they want, characters will use different strategies of communication. In David Mamet's *Sexual Perversity in Chicago,* a young woman who has just begun a love affair has been with her new boyfriend for several days. When she returns to the apartment she shares with a woman friend, her roommate greets her laconically: "Your plants died."

Instantly, we learn a good deal about the roommate's personality, the women's relationship, the passage of time, domestic responsibility, jealousy, and cynicism. In performance, this complex moment is poignant, and can be very funny.

Some characters don't talk much, but are devastatingly powerful. In Harold Pinter's *The Homecoming,* for instance, Ruth has few lines, but she is onstage a lot, observing, absorbing the male energy around her before vanquishing it with her own. Ruth dominates the play without expending anything like the verbal effort put forth by the other characters, who are trying to gain her favor; in performance, her seeming passivity is so active that it makes their activity seem passive!

Audiences tend to believe what stage characters say. You can use this credulity in many ways. One of your most interesting options is to have characters *lie*—to themselves, to other characters, and thus to the audience. Moreover, even characters who lie may also sometimes tell the truth—a situation ripe for dramatic exploitation.

Direct audience address

Frequently, in contemporary plays, characters talk directly to the audience, a technique that has mixed results. If one of your characters confides in the audience, make sure the character *has* to do so. After all, when a character speaks directly to the audience, the illusion of "the fourth wall"—the fiction that the audience observes the events of a play through an invisible but transparent barrier—is broken. This can be exhilarating, because the audience *is* in a theatre and knows at some level of consciousness that what they are watching is not reality itself, but a dramatic *representation* of reality.

However, it's best to use direct audience address sparingly. While there's no law against breaking any convention in the theatre, make sure that you are doing so for the right reasons. Don't have a character directly address the audience simply because it appears to be *easier* to tell the audience what it needs to know, rather than to show it. Telling is always easier than showing, but it is lazy playwriting. Your story will usually be more effectively dramatized by juxtaposing characters with different and conflicting agendas.

But not always.

Addressing an audience directly can at times be very useful for exposition—the "back story," as it's called in Hollywood—necessary to bring an audience up to speed quickly. Here's a classic example, the opening scene of Shakespeare's *Richard III*. Richard, Duke of Gloucester, tells the audience of his recent victory in the Wars of the Roses. Then he confides:

> But I,—that am not shap'd for sporting tricks,
> Nor made to court an amorous looking-glass;
> I, that am rudely stamp'd, and want love's majesty
> To strut before a wanton ambling nymph;
> I, that am curtail'd of this fair proportion,
> Cheated of feature by dissembling nature,
> Deform'd, unfinish'd, sent before my time
> Into this breathing world, scarce half made up,
> And that so lamely and unfashionable,

> That dogs bark at me, as I halt by them;—
> Why, I, in this weak piping time of peace,
> Have no delight to pass away the time;
> Unless to spy my shadow in the sun,
> And descant on mine own deformity:
> And therefore, since I cannot prove a lover,
> To entertain these fair well-spoken days,
> I am determined to prove a villain . . .

And he goes on to tell the audience something of the plots he has set in motion to secure the throne for himself.

Much of the information in this monologue could have been shown in a few scenes, rather than told in a speech, but Shakespeare chose instead to dramatize later events in Richard's life, with the "facts" above as background. Richard's speech serves several purposes: In very condensed form, he tells the audience about his misshapen body, about his ambition, about the tangled politics of England. He also reveals a savage intelligence and sense of irony, with deep feelings of betrayal, loss, and bitterness. Slyly, he also turns the audience into co-conspirators, accessories before the fact.

Here's a contemporary American example of the same technique, in David Rabe's *A Question of Mercy:*

> *The set is a raised, raked platform surrounded by a ground level alley that runs along stage right and left and across the front. The backdrop is abstract. Perhaps it suggests an urban skyline. Downstage left on the ground-floor ramp stands a table with a phone on it.*

> *There is music and a dreamy kind of light on Dr. Robert Chapman as he enters upstage left. He's in his forties, tall, and he walks down toward the table and chair. He wears an overcoat, which he unbuttons, then removes. He looks out to the audience, taking them in. He speaks as*

*if making a formal presentation on a supremely im-
portant issue.*

DR. CHAPMAN

This overcoat—my overcoat was given to me ten—no.
He's twenty-three now and he was ... so it's ... my
overcoat is fifteen years old. It was a Christmas gift
from my nephew. I'm sure it was really my sister who
purchased it. But my nephew was the bearer, his little
face a bright bulb above the festive package as he raced
across the room. *(Slightly puzzled but still grand, he
continues)* I don't know why I'm saying this. But I wear
it—the overcoat when I go out in cold weather. *(With the
overcoat in one hand, he turns to a pair of pajamas on
the chair)* These are my pajamas. *(Grabbing them up)*
At night, I wear them. They provide a kind of consoling
formality. *(He holds the pajamas in one hand, the overcoat
in the other, both arms outstretched as he weighs the
garments, his arms shifting like scales)* The boundary,
the demarcation between waking and sleeping, between
thought and dreams benefits, I believe, from such an
acknowledgment—a gesture of respect, of emphasis, I
think.

*The phone rings. The backdrop holds a projection, nar-
row and clear: JANUARY 9, 1990.*

This speech is very different from Richard's. Dr.
Chapman is a far less titanic character, and his preci-
sion (bordering on fussiness) is crucial to the moral
issue of the play that follows. By giving us a minor
personal revelation in a situation of public address, the
playwright intrigues us with the contrast between the
occasion and the information. We immediately want to
know more. Dr. Chapman is an ordinary man who will
have to make an extraordinary decision—whether or
not to participate in the mercy killing of an AIDS patient—with a mind and heart that instinctively shrink
from such decision-making. With quiet craftsmanship,

David Rabe reveals enough of the doctor's character to entice us, before he confronts him (and us) with the play's central challenge.

So, use any technique you like to introduce a character, as long as the technique is both revealing and compelling. The issue is not whether "it's been done," but whether *you* are doing it well.

Villains and other unsavory characters

Shakespeare made Richard III the protagonist as well as the villain, which brings up another point about character. Some audiences complain when they encounter characters they don't like, who are not "nice," who do nasty things to other people. It used to be a convention in plays—and *Richard III* is no exception—to reveal such characters in all their vicious glory, then have them get their comeuppance. Richard, after all, is killed in hand-to-hand combat, screaming, "A horse! A horse! My kingdom for a horse!"

Nowadays, there's no guarantee that the audience will have the satisfaction of seeing unsavory characters "get theirs." In fact, such retribution in a modern play would be considered too hokey, too conveniently moralistic, too far from observable reality, for the audience to accept it. Nevertheless, today's audiences are often troubled by characters who are angry or violent, or otherwise perceived as threatening the audience's view of the world and way of life. Len Jenkin's *Five of Us* is an excellent play which, in its pursuit of a higher truth, risks alienating audiences, as does David Mamet's *Edmond*. Both plays are good examples of first-rate scripts with troublesome themes—and a refusal by the playwrights even to acknowledge an audience's desire for the satisfaction of retribution. Troubling? Sure. But any play that subverts our natural complacency by raising primal issues—and does so well—deserves special recognition.

It's not important that your audience *like* your characters; it is important that they accept their existence, allowing them to be who they are in the context you have created for them. There is a great temptation these days to soften characters, to make them palatable and therefore bland. You should resist this temptation.

Tony Kushner's fascinating, powerful portrayal of Roy Cohn in *Angels in America* illustrates this point perfectly. The real Roy Cohn was surely a loathsome human being, and Kushner's dramatic recreation of him makes that clear. But the character is *alive*, full of nasty energy. Watching him is like seeing Satan at play. You hate him, but you can't take your eyes off him. The audience can watch this man lie, manipulate others, and defy his own imminent death—and be perfectly safe as they do so.

Avoid making your characters "politically correct." While the impulse to create open-hearted, open-minded egalitarian drama is noble, it can backfire, and the result is predictable and boring. Your play may require your characters to say or do things that you or others would find inappropriate. After all, if human beings did nothing wrong, stupid, or gross, there wouldn't be much theatre. The great characters of the drama, both classical and modern, are often quite impossible, or would be in real life. But theatre is *not* real life.

Don't be afraid to create characters whose language, points of view, and behavior you don't agree with. Naïve audiences may waste their time trying to figure out which character(s) speak for you; more sophisticated audiences know that in a good play *all* the characters "speak for" the playwright, yet are not the playwright. You can create characters you love, and characters you'd never want anywhere near you. Put them together! See what happens! Just make them all memorable, tough, complex.

What if you need a truly saintly character in your play? This is not as easy as creating an interesting villain. We are suspicious of saints. Making a saintly person credible on stage is a true challenge, so difficult that few playwrights have succeeded at it—but it is possible. Saintliness, like other traits, must be seen through action, or it remains passive, theoretical, and unpersuasive. Therefore, the most effective way to create such a character is to dramatize the struggle he or she has with various temptations to be less than saintly. That way, saintliness won't be dismissed as a static, dull condition, but will be seen instead as the result of believable inner conflict. It will appear more human, and therefore more credible.

It's usually unwise to have a character state the theme of your play, or even to suggest that the stage story *has* a theme. Focus instead on what the characters *want* and on what actions they must take to achieve it. The audience will then have all the information it needs to perceive the theme clearly.

Don't have your characters explain their motivations. Plays in which characters speak as though they've had years of psychotherapy tend to be dramatically inert, because they do too much of the audience's work, too little of their own. Such plays often rely on therapeutic jargon, which has its uses in the appropriate context, but in the theatre can sound smug and simplistic. You may find this useful if you're writing a satire like Christopher Durang's *Beyond Therapy,* but a serious drama with a psychological dimension requires a different verbal strategy for your characters.

Fortunately, the language of "ordinary" people is perfectly adequate for revealing character. Imagine someone whose every statement is a platitude. What emotions, what needs, underlie the constant use of prefabricated language? Anyone who takes refuge in a stream of clichés will certainly be annoying; he or she may also, on occasion, be acute. Such a character can have multiple uses in your play, even occasionally as a source of unexpected wisdom. Under what conditions would such a person truly speak from the heart? Questions like these will help you define your characters as they should be defined—by their behavior.

Think of your cast of characters as an orchestra—whether chamber, symphony, *klezmer* or jug band doesn't matter. Much of your play's "music" comes from the permutations and combinations of characters as they speak and interact, so mixing speakers with different voices and rhythms automatically creates a theatrical "score."

As your play evolves, any kind of change in a character is permissible, as long as he or she behaves consistently within the parameters that you set. As you move from draft to draft, altering a character's age, gender, education, or social class will have an impact on both the story and the other characters in the play. Adding, deleting, and combining characters may follow. Ask yourself whether such changes make each of your characters and your story less stereotypical, more distinctive, and does each change *raise the dramatic stakes?*

Every alteration will force you to review your dialogue, and usually to revise and tighten it. Once your characters are established *verbally*—that is, with their conflicting personalities revealed by their particular and unique ways of speaking—keep in mind that, on stage, they also exist *visually*. That raises quite a different set of challenges.

2. The *non-verbal*

Since you're writing for performance, you need to think about *people*—not just about words on a page; about non-verbal communication; and about communication in three dimensions.

While words are important, visual elements, silence, and non-verbal sounds all should be part of your playwriting strategy. Words express only what characters *say*. An actor's tone of voice, speech rhythms, and body language express in a more complex way the emotions that underlie a character's words. This is what actors call "subtext." What's *between* the lines may reinforce what's being said out loud, or contradict it. In either case, what *isn't* spoken may well be more important to the effectiveness of your play than what *is*.

The 18th-century English diarist Samuel Pepys often wrote of going to the theatre "to hear a play." We don't do that any more; nowadays, we go to *see* a play. The difference is crucial. For us, seeing is believing. Therefore, in the theatre, where the entire visual and aural context can be manipulated for effect, gestures and non-verbal sounds can contribute to an audience's understanding of character as strongly as the playwright's words. You need to appreciate what non-verbal communication can and cannot do to define your characters. How do they walk? Do they belch? When? If they turned on the radio, would they tune it to classical music? Golden oldies? A talk show? Or would they surf the airwaves impatiently?

Combining verbal and non-verbal techniques will reveal a character far more effectively than either mode alone. In Maria Irene Fornés's play *The Conduct of*

Life, for example, an exploited domestic servant in the household of a Latin American fascist talks to us as she works. She lists a number of things she does as soon as she wakes up, adding, "Then I start the day." After another list of chores, she repeats, "Then I start the day." After a third list, she says it again. And we're exhausted!

We understand, we *feel,* the dreariness of this character's life, and the oppression of her situation, even as we see her do her chores quickly and efficiently. The playwright's words and the actress's physical actions combine to create an unforgettable character, and drama with a powerful political sensibility.

3. The *interrelational*
I've been talking about character as if each personality in a play were an individual, distinct from other characters and more or less independent of them. But characters in plays are even less autonomous than human beings are in the "real" world. Whatever the rules of the dramatic universe you've created may be, chances are that *relationships* between and among characters are more important to the play's energy and drive than any individual character you create can ever be.

Therefore, try to think about your characters in significant pairs, in crucial triangles, in the context of their society, as well as individually. You can create character groupings that illustrate the workings of social forces, without being too obvious, without losing the charm of the immediate and personal. If required by your script, you can alter audience expectations of time, space, blood ties, cause and effect, or anything else that is usually taken for granted. This is fun to do, and it stops conventional thinking in its tracks—one of the reasons we need theatre in the first place.

British playwright Caryl Churchill's *Cloud 9,* for example, subverts commonplace notions of what character *is,* in the theatre and in the world. Her highly economical method, which only a truly imaginative playwright could use so effectively, explodes received ideas about gender and its immutability by having men play female roles and women play male roles, all of whom interact in highly provocative ways. The playwright dramatizes complex issues that range from patriarchy and imperialism to domestic violence and sexual pleasure. The play is exhilarating, because Caryl Churchill has the wit and the craft to turn audience expectations of character upside down—and make them like the result.

One of the most influential characters in dramatic literature never appears on stage! No, I'm not talking about Samuel Beckett's elusive Godot. The character I mean is called Protopopov, and he is Natasha's offstage lover in Anton Chekhov's *Three Sisters.* We never see him; we learn only secondhand who he is and what he does to (and for) the Prozorov family. Read the play, and trace his effect on what happens. Some critics consider him a home-wrecking villain; others think that he treats the Prozorovs better than they have any right to expect. Both views may be true. Consider using an offstage character as a powerful dramatic device in *your* play.

Sometimes audiences will question the extreme actions that characters take. Sometimes other characters will speak for that audience. Henrik Ibsen's *Hedda Gabler* contains the perfect example: Judge Brack, whose response to Hedda's suicide is, "Good God—people don't *do* such things!" But we have seen, step by step, as Judge Brack has not, the sequence of events that makes Hedda's suicide plausible and memorable.

It's not uncommon for actors to question whether or not "their" character would say such-and-such. Listen to them—they may have a point—but they may not. A well-known actor in a starring role in a television series that featured a talking dolphin insisted on rewriting the animal's lines, arguing, "The dolphin wouldn't say that." In the theatre, these choices are made by the playwright.

Playwrights obviously don't use every technique they know to present character, but your own arsenal of methods for making the people in your play "work" is bound to grow, whether you write kitchen-sink realism, post-neo-futurist cabaret sketches, playlets for children, or any other dramatic form that puts human beings on a stage. As you learn and master contemporary techniques that fulfill your needs, you will also encounter older techniques that you can update to suit your purposes. And, of course, you should feel free to invent your own. Whatever makes your characters memorable makes *you* a better playwright.

❖❖ 3

Transforming Story
into Plot

W HAT *IS* A PLOT, anyway? What's the difference between a plot and a story? And how do you create
one from another?

Here's a classic distinction: "The queen died, and then
the king died" is a story. "The queen died, and then the
king died *of grief*" is a plot. *Story,* then, is the events
of a play, in whatever order you choose to tell them.
Plot concerns the relationship among these events and
the characters who enact them.

We can infer that our king and queen had more than
a political marriage, that their public relationship con-
tained (and probably concealed) a powerful emotional
bond. In such a case, our hypothetical king's death may
be explained to his subjects as an emotional response
to the loss of his queen. How sad! How moving! But
what if, behind the scenes, a darker political struggle
is taking place? What if the king's death means the end
of one dynasty and the establishment of another, with
a civil war to decide which dynasty will rule? Yes, the
king's grief was deep, but did it *really* cause his death?

Or was it a convenient coincidence? As Shakespeare put it (cynically): "Men have died from time to time, and worms have eaten them; but not for love." Then how *did* the king die? For that matter, how did the *queen* die? What if . . . ? Or could the king's grief and a political struggle be *simultaneous truths?* Of course they could.

As you see, the dramatic possibilities inherent in this situation are limitless.

In such a case, plot and character influence each other in many ways, and as the playwright, you determine which influences are most important.

As a practical matter, the story of your play is likely to develop well before its plot does, because all the linkages among events and characters—both obvious and subtle—that make up an effective plot are usually a result of several drafts. Getting the story elements right, and presenting them in the most effective order, is hard enough; but making a plot out of the story, a plot in which every moment gives just enough information and no more, in which the play's forward movement is both unmistakable and compelling, is even harder.

Fortunately, the complicated and lengthy process of creating a play from an idea, or an image, or a character, or whatever you start from, is ultimately more fascinating than frustrating. Don't worry if your plot isn't completely clear to you at the outset. Don't worry if you don't know all there is to know about each character before you start writing your script. Some playwrights create random lists of character traits, then sculpt each list into a person. Try this, and see if it works for you. Or you may be more comfortable imagining a character as a whole, and discovering additional traits as they reveal themselves in the course of your writing the play.

Alternatively, you may start with an event, then say, "What kind of character would most likely be involved in such an event?" Or (and better), "What kind of character would be highly *un*likely to be involved in such an event, and what would happen if he or she *were* so involved?"

In your first draft, feel free to begin with bits and pieces of your story. Don't worry, at this point, about unity, coherence, or emphasis. Step by step, make each event or transaction into a scene; each scene into a series of scenes that fit together according to your dramatic vision; each series of scenes into an act; each act into a play. Take your time, building the overall structure out of smaller units. You need not write the play in chronological order. In later drafts, you can cut, add, rearrange, expand, contract—do whatever is necessary to make those bits and pieces fit together seamlessly.

Motion

Traditionally, a play is supposed to have a beginning, a middle, and an end; plays that do so are highly satisfying to most audiences. But you can make an arbitrary choice of where in a story to start and where to end. Those choices will define the middle. Remember, you can always use a *flashback* or *flash-forward,* as the structure of your play may require.

One common test for the effectiveness of a play is whether or not it has *forward motion,* but while *most* plays need to move forward through time with some urgency, there are some really great plays that do not. Their motion is circular or spiral, their force centripetal. Their action meanders, and their characters seem stuck in time and place.

Consider Anton Chekhov's plays, in which the leisure of the landed Russian gentry conceals a dim, anguished perception that nothing they do will keep their world from coming to an end. A lot happens in Chekhov, but it tends to happen *offstage*. Chekhov dramatizes a world that seems to have no drama, except for the occasional intense moment; deftly, he turns the typical plot-rich 19th-century play into examinations of character so subtle, yet so powerful, that generations of actors have found exploring roles in his plays to be indispensable for their training. Chekhov's plays don't have much forward motion in the traditional sense, because they reveal a world that is autumnal, burnt out, yet they manage to proceed to their dramatically logical end with seemingly effortless grace.

Nevertheless, many dramatic authors today, and many audiences, expect a play to move forward clearly and quickly, partly because they have been conditioned by thousands of hours of film and television to mistake *action* for *drama*. In our daily lives, we learn to experience time primarily as linear. In our dreams, however, we experience time in many other ways, so plays with dream-like, imaginative structures tend to be less linear than plays that attempt to replicate the recognizable external world. Hamlet says that the purpose of theatre is "to hold, as 'twere, the mirror up to nature." You, the playwright, get to decide what sort of mirror, and what aspect of nature. For example, Harold Pinter's *Betrayal* begins after its events have taken place, and tells its story backwards. The audience experiences how memory revises our lives, and how actions that destroy human relationships may begin in a chance word here, a careless gesture there. In a different mode, Tennessee Williams created *The Glass Menagerie* consciously as a dream play. Time swirls, history repeats itself, "real" objects become symbols, and so on. On stage, private dreams may become public magic.

Most playwrights follow a "forward motion" model, in which story elements are kept or discarded to the degree that they move the plot toward its climax and conclusion. Forward motion gathers momentum, so that a play seems to move faster and faster as it nears its most revealing moment. This is the technique Sophocles used in as early a play as *Oedipus Rex:* He created the sensation of increasing speed by making each successive scene shorter (and therefore more intense) than the preceding one, until the play's ultimate, inexorable revelation.

Sophocles' invention is thoroughly adaptable to our time. *Glengarry Glen Ross,* David Mamet's feisty, funny play about sleazy Chicago real-estate salesmen, is an excellent contemporary example of the Sophoclean model of forward motion—and yet Sophocles is probably the last influence you'll think of if you read or see Mamet's play. *Glengarry's* combination of verbal jazz, lean structure, and ruthless analysis of petty capitalism seems utterly American and up-to-date.

This is an important reason for you to acquaint yourself with as many plays as possible. Imagine using a 2,500-year-old technique for thoroughly modern purposes! There's no need to reinvent the wheel, but rediscovering what makes it turn can be very helpful to any playwright.

Sometimes a plot is described in terms of "rising action," "climax," and "falling action," generally to show how dramatic stories move from A to B to C. Plays structured this way often have impressive power and clarity, but not all viable dramatic paths are linear. These days, more and more dramatic material that is fragmented, or repetitive in subtle ways, or is simply a series of blackout sketches, finds its way to successful performance. Nevertheless, because "forward motion" has such power over us, many playwrights' work is criticized for what it *doesn't do* rather than appreciated for what it *does* — especially if the play's motion is seemingly static. Any play, no matter how much it seems to hold an objective mirror up to everyday reality, is in fact an imaginative creation in which the playwright has the option of reaffirming the commonly accepted rules of time, space, and behavior, or inventing new ones. Whatever the playwright's choice, the more consistently and tellingly these rules are applied, the more persuasive the play will be.

Plays that appear to be about the world we all share are easier to appreciate than plays about worlds that exist only in the writer's mind, but of course this depends on the writer. August Strindberg worked quite effectively in both modes. *The Father* is ruthlessly objective, while *The Ghost Sonata* is much more obviously a dream play. The same dark comic sensibility informs both dramas, but in the first, forward motion is relentless. In the second, motion comes in many diverse forms. If you compare these texts to Canadian playwright George F. Walker's *Suburban Motel* cycle, you'll see how forward motion and circular repetition can be combined. I wouldn't have thought of mixing together the sensibilities of Sam Shepard and the Marx Brothers, but Walker did, and the result is wacky, preposterous theatre with a great core of human truth.

If your talent is for writing non-linear and/or non-realistic plays, it's up to you to provide alternate sources of dramatic energy. Here are a few such sources: progressive revelation of character (e.g., Emily Mann's *Still Life*), increasing emotional intensity (e.g., Sam Shepard's *Buried Child*), more powerful imagery of states of inertia (e.g. Samuel Beckett's *Happy Days*), vivid theatrical poetry (e.g. Federico Garcia Lorca's *Blood Wedding*). *Something* has to take the place of forward motion, or your play will be wan and tepid.

You can, of course, combine linear and non-linear elements in your play, or realistic scenes and non-realistic scenes. This sort of dramatic counterpoint has exciting theatrical possibilities.

There are many techniques that will help you turn your story into a plot:

1. *Follow your instincts about which elements of your story deserve the most stage time.*

2. *As you draft and redraft, you will notice patterns emerging in your story. Make linkages among these patterns through the repetition and development of language, symbols, and sounds, as appropriate to the characters and situation—so that you are working on verbal, visual, and aural dimensions of your play simultaneously.* How does Shakespeare use the witches in *Macbeth* to create atmosphere, provide information, and dramatize the interplay between the ordinary and the occult? How does David Mamet's *American Buffalo* make verbal repetition and the focus on small rituals coexist in a wholly appropriate and resonant context? Read Mamet's description of the play's setting, and notice how the setting and the dialogue complement each other.

3. *If your plot is starting to feel too convoluted, try "storyboarding" it.* Borrow a technique from film writing: Put units of action on index cards, then put each index card on your wall. Does the first way you arranged each card make sense to you? Do you need all the cards?

Are there gaps in the pattern? If so, do you need to fill these gaps? How can you rearrange the cards so that a different, perhaps more provocative, pattern begins to emerge? Follow that trail!

4. *As the playwright, only you know which events in the early part of a play will in retrospect be seen as significant.* Theatre people refer to such an event as a *setup*. To complete the structural (and emotional) circle, a setup must be followed, usually at some distance, by a *payoff*. This is usually some sort of surprise, some event or revelation that in retrospect is inevitable, without having been predictable in advance. Oscar Wilde's preposterous coincidences, late in *The Importance of Being Earnest,* are wonderful examples of payoffs, absurd and delightful at the same time.

Make sure, therefore, that your setups stay concealed, but don't forget that there must be a payoff—unless you choose, for some good reason, *not* to pay off a setup, to leave the structural-emotional circle unclosed. To look at it from another angle: In writing a payoff, make sure that you go back and locate the setup. If there isn't one, invent one. Then hide it.

Hidden setups that are paid off openly and tellingly occur in Edward Albee's *Who's Afraid of Virginia Woolf?,* when the offstage child is revealed as a fantasy with the emotional impact of reality; in Shakespeare's *Macbeth,* when Birnam Wood *does* come to Dunsinane, though not in the form we expect; and in Bertolt Brecht's *Mother Courage,* when the significance of Swiss Cheese's nickname becomes chillingly clear.

5. *What can you cut without weakening your play's structure?* If your first answer is "Nothing!"—look again.

6. *Be careful about #5.* August Wilson's plays, such as *Fences, The Piano Lesson,* and *Seven Guitars,* are characterized by a loose, open architecture and a lot of rambling discourse that can seem repetitive and verbose. But since Wilson is dramatizing a culture with a complicated attitude about time and how best to pass it, it makes some sense for his plays to unfold slowly, with a lot of fits and starts and blind alleys. The rough edges of Wilson's writing, the meandering and curlicues, become attributes of an identifiable individual *style* of playwriting. This style may not be suitable for every playwright, but it is an artistic choice.

In other words, don't be too quick to homogenize your work. You have a right to your idiosyncrasies; in the end, they may be more valuable than you expected.

7. *There is a certain satisfaction to tying up all the loose ends of a play neatly, as in the much-abused, little-appreciated "well-made" play; but this sort of tightly contrived and controlled playwriting has few advocates today.* It survives most obviously in TV sitcoms and movies. A looser structure seems to suit many contemporary playwrights. There may be a greater satisfaction in leaving some elements unresolved, so that the audience is left wanting to know what happens to the characters even after the play is over. This is more like life itself, in which few questions are answered totally and unambiguously.

For example, in Arthur Miller's *Death of a Salesman,* the author focuses most of our attention on Willy Loman, his (anti)hero. But this major focus is buttressed by a strong secondary focus on Willy's family. What happens to Linda, Biff, and Happy after Willy's suicide? We never really learn, so part of the significance of Willy's choice is lost to us. But, you can't write about everything at once. Choosing *which* elements to leave unresolved is the mark of a master, and this mastery is the result of practice.

After reading *Death of a Salesman,* read Donald Margulies' *The Loman Family Picnic.* There's a lesson here about the constructive use of an older play to inspire a new one, and the illumination of the older play by the newer one. Tom Stoppard's plays *Rosencrantz and Guildenstern are Dead, The Real Inspector Hound,* and *Travesties* are both tributes to and parodies of, respectively, Shakespeare's *Hamlet,* any Agatha Christie murder mystery, and Oscar Wilde's *The Importance of Being Earnest.* The most significant fact to keep in mind, though, is that each of Stoppard's plays stands perfectly well on its own. You don't need to have read or seen the plays that inspired them, but if you have, you get an extra measure of enjoyment from the echoes, and can learn from the ways this approach has been used.

8. *Make your exposition serve multiple purposes. Exposition* is information about characters and events from the past or present that an audience needs to know to appreciate onstage action fully.

Although audiences *want* to know what's going on at every moment, they don't *need* to know. Suspense is an important attribute in a play, because it reinforces an audience's curiosity and helps provide some of the forward motion. So when should you provide vital information? For many purposes, at the latest possible moment. This does *not* mean that you save all crucial information until the play's last five minutes, then tell the audience everything you've withheld; but make sure you've explored indirect ways of giving information before you do so directly.

One of the most effective ways to do this is to have your characters discuss what actions they are *going to* take, rather than what they have done in the past. You'll find that any necessary background or character information will emerge organically, so that you don't have to slow your play down by giving the audience chunks of history.

In contemporary plays, exposition is almost never *just* exposition; it often contains action as well as other kinds of information. Emily Mann's *Execution of Justice* dramatizes the famous and controversial murder trial of Dan White, the San Francisco politician who shot Mayor George Moscone and gay activist Harvey Milk in 1975. The play's strategy is to give us a kaleidoscopic view of the community in which it takes place. The profusion and sprawl of actual events, the candid reminiscences of people involved in the trial, and volumes of court testimony are all challenges to the playwright's need for dramatic economy. They were also her raw material.

Given this complexity, every moment in *Execution of Justice* had to serve several purposes simultaneously. The drama opens with two characters speaking. They are both onstage, close to each other, yet they seldom acknowledge each other's presence. They represent two opposing factions in the community and in the play. One of the characters is an unnamed San Francisco policeman who wears a "Free Dan White" T-shirt under his uniform; the other is Sister Boom-Boom, a gay transvestite in a nun's habit. From the first moment of the play, we are confronted with a kind of civic schizophrenia. The scene sets the tone for the play, and introduces us to its larger subject: the conflict of different value systems within the same community. It is exposition disguised as action.

You may never confront the challenge of effective exposition to such a degree in your own work, but *Execution of Justice* is a good example of how to rise to such a challenge.

9. *"Show, don't tell" means don't say directly in words what you can convey indirectly through behavior, and never, ever sermonize.* This is generally gospel for contemporary playwrights. But, as Sportin' Life says of that *other* gospel, "It ain't necessarily so." There are exceptions. Look at Tony Kushner's play *Slavs! (Thinking About the Problems of Virtue and Happiness)* for a recent example of "breaking the rules" and getting away with it. This play begins with a character reading to the audience out of a book! There are few clearer ways of saying outright, "Let's save time. This is what you need to know." I admire the playwright's nerve, his willingness to do whatever he felt the situation required, and "show, don't tell" be damned. You may never start a play with a lecture, and I hope that doing so never becomes fashionable; but it *is* part of the available stock of playwriting strategies.

There are many ways of turning a story—whether totally fictional or taken from headlines like *Execution of Justice*—into a plot, then into a play. Whether character, structure, theatricality, or mood predominates depends very much on choices you make and the sort of effect you are trying to achieve: Even the most rigid dramatic structure is really quite malleable.

Consider, for example, what Ibsen did with the "well-made" play of his time, and what Shakespeare did with the Elizabethan dramatic forms he inherited. Look at the idiosyncratic contemporary comedies of the late Charles Ludlam, plays such as *Camille (A Tearjerker), Der Ring Gott Farblonjet, Le Bourgeois Avant-Garde,*

The Mystery of Irma Vep—unique, yet clearly inspired by such older dramatic forms as Restoration comedy and Victorian melodrama. Bertolt Brecht was famous for updating older dramatic structures into contemporary forms. His *Mother Courage* and *The Caucasian Chalk Circle,* for example, revised an open, Shakespearean, "epic" way of writing plays. Don't be afraid to mine the past for intriguing ways to turn your stories into play plots. Don't be afraid to invent new ways to do so, either.

❖❖ 4

"A Good Ear for Dialogue"

I N REAL LIFE, we get a lot of information from other people through the words they speak, their body language, tone of voice, speech rhythms, and so on. This mixed-media communication is even more crucial in the theatre. "Dialogue" isn't just the words that characters speak; it's how the words are said, by whom, to whom, in what order, and for what purpose. Mastering the art of creating dialogue—what is sometimes called having a distinct "voice"—is crucial for your development as a playwright.

Some years ago, I was walking through New York's Central Park and ran into David Mamet, who was just becoming well-known in the American theatre. We chatted briefly, and he told me that he had an earache and was going to see a specialist. Then he grinned and said, "Don't worry. It's not the one for dialogue."

"A good ear for dialogue" is a common phrase of approval for a playwright's ability to create pungent and persuasive dramatic conversations, and Mamet's "ear" has been widely praised. But it may not be such a compliment. The implication is that playwrights don't invent the conversations in their scripts; they overhear them. George Bernard Shaw's delightful one-act *The Dark Lady of the Sonnets* dramatizes this notion by suggesting that Shakespeare's most memorable lines were the result of his eavesdropping on different London types, ranging from night watchmen to Queen Elizabeth herself.

Many playwrights do listen to the conversations of others, but I suspect they discard a great deal more than they use. It's more likely that playwrights invent most of their dialogue, then season it with bits and pieces from the actual day-to-day world. Consider this dramatic moment:

(Two teenagers, NATALIE and BRENDA, are walking down a city street. It is snowing.)

NATALIE

Un—

BRENDA

—believable!

NATALIE & BRENDA
(together)

Unbelievable.

NATALIE

What a dork.

BRENDA

What a jerk!

NATALIE

Totally. He's . . . oh, shit.

BRENDA

What?

NATALIE
I just stepped in some dog poo.

I overheard this conversation in the street, about a block from my house in Toronto, in early 1998. Its vivid economy and clear character revelation impressed me. I don't know the two young women; I never saw them before, so I have chosen names for them. Starting from this real-life exchange, I could write an entire play, and so could you. But "real-life exchanges" quickly give way to the imaginary exchanges that must follow. Street remarks may inspire you, but you'll have to fill in the blanks yourself. After all, I invented some of the above conversation. I alone know which part I made up.

What *is* dialogue, anyway?

Dialogue literally means a conversation between two people, but in the theatre the term includes all verbal exchanges in a play—monologues, choral speeches, asides, soliloquies, conversations, and so on. It is the primary means of theatrical communication.

One thing to remember about dialogue is that you can do quite a lot with very little. For example, in Tom Stoppard's political comedy *Travesties* (set in Zurich during World War I), the following conversation takes place between Henry Carr, a British diplomat, and Bennett, his valet:

BENNETT
I have put the newspapers and telegrams on the sideboard, sir.

CARR
Is there anything of interest?

BENNETT
There is a revolution in Russia, sir.

CARR
Really? What sort of revolution?

BENNETT
A social revolution, sir.

CARR
A *social* revolution? Unaccompanied women smoking at the opera, that sort of thing? . . .

At this point, we laugh. We understand clearly who Carr is, the nature of the society he's used to, and his languid incomprehension of a radically changing world. Stoppard tells us almost everything we need to know about this character *in one line*. But the playwright is not just revealing one character; he continues to move his comedy forward, giving us information about Bennett (who is a good deal brighter than Carr) and about the world of the play, in a wonderfully tight and focused exchange:

BENNETT
Not precisely that, sir. It is more in the nature of a revolution of classes contraposed by the fissiparous disequilibrium of Russian society.

CARR
What do you mean, classes?

BENNETT
Masters and servants. As it were. Sir.

CARR
Oh. Masters and servants. *Classes.*

BENNETT
(*expressionless as always*)
There have been scenes of violence.

CARR

I see. Well, I'm not in the least surprised, Bennett. I don't wish to appear wise after the event, but anyone with half an acquaintance with Russian society could see that the day was not far off before the exploited class, disillusioned by the neglect of its interests, alarmed by the falling value of the ruble, and above all goaded beyond endurance by the insolent rapacity of its servants, should turn upon those butlers, footmen, cooks, valets . . . .

Note that Carr does not ask Bennett to clarify what he means by "fissiparous disequilibrium," but rather, what he means by a much simpler concept: social classes. It then looks for a moment as if Carr will surprise us with his sympathy for the oppressed, until we realize that the joke's on us, as Stoppard flips Carr's expression of understanding upside down. Here, Stoppard uses comic dialogue to make a telling point about a wider social phenomenon: the great inability of those in power to comprehend the frustrations of the powerless.

In the tradition of Oscar Wilde and George Bernard Shaw, Tom Stoppard has the ability to distill major social insight into an accessible comedic format. If you have ever had the good fortune to see a Lily Tomlin performance, either live or on video, you will have observed a similar ability to create character and even action through witty, clever dialogue. In Tomlin's case, the dialogue comes from her close collaboration with playwright Jane Wagner.

It is worth studying the works of these playwrights to see how effortless they make their dialogue look and sound. But of course it is not effortless at all. What we read or see is the result of talent plus a lot of hard work.

Dialogue traps

You must be both cautious and bold in writing dialogue, while being careful not to fall into one of the great traps that lie in wait for the unwary dramatist: *too much cleverness.* Who among us has not written a line, or even an entire speech, and laughed at our own wit, or marveled at our brilliantly expressed insight into the human condition? You think that others will be similarly impressed, that the more witty the comments you put into your characters' mouths, the better chance of having your play produced and acclaimed. If you are Noël Coward, Christopher Durang, Tom Stoppard, Wendy Wasserstein, or Oscar Wilde—writers who generally transcend the limitations of witty stage chat—this may be the case, but not all playwrights are as gifted.

Nevertheless, an ability to write one-liners and to have your characters speak them at dramatically appropriate moments is admirable. Thanks to the popularity of television sitcoms and stand-up comedians, there is a large market for light comedies and farces, especially in the commercial theatre. But as you create characters, keep in mind that too much wit can seem self-conscious and brittle, a superficial substitute for the true communication you may be seeking. Sometimes, when you're watching a play and are absorbed in it, a character will suddenly say something that seems to come directly from the playwright, rather than naturally from the character. Immediately, the illusion of character is destroyed, and the play then moves on without taking the audience with it.

I once heard a playwriting teacher suggest that you should find all the "great lines" in your script and take them out! I wouldn't go that far, principally because I don't think you should ever avoid using any dramatic tool that you find useful; but wit is a spice best sprinkled, not poured.

Another trap to avoid is *too much* dialogue.

How much is too much?

This is a judgment call, and it's your responsibility as the playwright to make the judgment. Here are a few practical questions you can ask yourself:

1. As you read a speech, several exchanges among characters, or whole scenes, *are there places where you sense a loss of energy, where the play seems to lose focus, slow down, or stand still?*

These are clear signs that the section is overwritten. Take a closer look: Are you giving only the information that is necessary to keep the play moving? Could you condense or move a section to a better place in the play? Try to isolate the reason *why* you feel this slowdown. That will help you find the way to fix it. Remember: If *you* notice a loss of focus, chances are an audience will, too.

2. *Are you repeating yourself?*

Are your characters saying the same things to each other several times, possibly in different words, but with the same emotional dynamics? If so, why? Make sure this kind of repetition is made for good dramatic reason. Here's an example, from a play that recently received a developmental workshop at Toronto's Cahoots Theatre Projects.

Canadian novelist Stephen Reid's first play, *Doing the Book,* is set in a men's prison. Bobby, the main character, is telling Victor Prettywoman, a new inmate, about his plans to escape with his weightlifter friend Meat:

                      BOBBY
You might as well know from jump street. *(Beat)* Me
and Meat are making a move.

(BOBBY sees the need, so he spells it out.)

We're escaping.

                   PRETTYWOMAN
Now? This minute?

*(BOBBY sits down, produces a pack of playing cards
and shuffles them expertly.)*

                      BOBBY
Relax. There's a lot of Preparation H yet. We've done
this before.

                   PRETTYWOMAN
With limited success, obviously.

                      BOBBY
Shut up. Meat's got a plan. You play that guitar while
we cut the bars, then one night all three of us will duck
out of here.

*(BOBBY fans the cards across the table, in perfect
order.)*

                   PRETTYWOMAN
I think I'll probably wait out my appeal if it's all the
same.

*(PRETTYWOMAN picks up the end card, runs it edge-
wise along the fan, lifting up and dropping the cards
expertly.)*

But I'll help you in any way I can. I should show you
my trick with the three kings. Simplest thing in the
world. Any idiot could do it.

BOBBY

Ahem. Let's just concentrate on this first. *(Beat)* This penitentiary is built, man. Them walls are four feet thick. They go forty feet into the ground. The bars are an inch and a quarter through. They were made in the old days, hammered by hand, and tempered in hell. *(Beat)* You don't break out of this place, you wear it down.

PRETTYWOMAN

I'd be willing to help.

(MEAT, using just a forefinger and a thumb, measures PRETTYWOMAN's bicep)

MEAT

You play music, we'll cut.

(BOBBY, trying to adjust the TV, bangs it with the side of his hand)

BOBBY

Sometimes I'll be out here with you, sometimes Meat. *(Beat)* Here, unscrew that cable.

(BOBBY exits into "One South." PRETTYWOMAN un-screws the cable. MEAT picks up the leather and re-sumes lacing.)

MEAT

Keeps my fingers nimble.

PRETTYWOMAN

You given this much thought? About where you'll go. What you'll do?

MEAT

That's Bobby's job. I just want to go someplace where the water's warm and all the fish look like they've been painted. *(Beat)* Maybe you should play a little on that guitar, get Trapdoor used to it.

> PRETTYWOMAN
> *(strums awkwardly)*
> How'd he get the name Trapdoor?

> MEAT
> We say it 'cause it bugs him, mostly. *(Beat)* Supposed
> to be a story he was the last hangman.

> PRETTYWOMAN
> Him?

> MEAT
> Why not. All you got to do is close your eyes and pull a
> lever. I don't know, ask Bobby, he's been here the longest.

> *(PRETTYWOMAN plays disjointedly.)*

> You're not very good at that, are you?

> PRETTYWOMAN
> I always wanted to learn, promised myself I would
> in here.

> MEAT
> You'll be José fucken Feliciano time you finish that
> nickel. *(Beat)* I'm gonna go see what it looks like down
> there.

None of the writing in this scene is bad writing, but
some of the information given is slightly repetitious,
and could be deleted with no loss to the play. Some of
the information is necessary, but would function more
effectively if moved to another scene. An essential question of script editing is: *How does what is here affect
the play's forward motion?*

The scene above comes from the draft of Reid's play
with which the Cahoots workshop began. Here's the
excerpt again, with my suggestions for cuts in boldface:

BOBBY

You might as well know from jump street. *(Beat)* Me and Meat are making a move.

(BOBBY sees the need, so he spells it out.)

We're escaping.

PRETTYWOMAN

Now? This minute?

(BOBBY sits down, produces a pack of playing cards and shuffles them expertly.)

BOBBY

Relax. There's a lot of Preparation H yet. We've done this before.

PRETTYWOMAN

With limited success, obviously.

BOBBY

Shut up. Meat's got a plan. You play that guitar while we cut the bars, then one night all three of us will duck out of here.

(BOBBY fans the cards across the table, in perfect order.)

PRETTYWOMAN

I think I'll probably wait out my appeal if it's all the same.

(PRETTYWOMAN picks up the end card, runs it edgewise along the fan, lifting up and dropping the cards expertly.)

But I'll help you in any way I can. **I should show you my trick with the three kings. Simplest thing in the world. Any idiot could do it.**

BOBBY
Ahem. Let's just concentrate on this first. *(Beat)*
This penitentiary is built, man. Them walls are
four feet thick. They go forty feet into the ground.
The bars are an inch and a quarter through. They
were made in the old days, hammered by hand,
and tempered in hell. *(Beat)* **You don't break out**
of this place, you wear it down.

PRETTYWOMAN
I'd be willing to help.

(MEAT, using just a forefinger and a thumb, measures
PRETTYWOMAN's bicep.)

MEAT
You play music, we'll cut.

(BOBBY, trying to adjust the TV, bangs it with the side
of his hand.)

BOBBY
Sometimes I'll be out here with you, sometimes Meat.
(Beat) Here, unscrew that cable.

(BOBBY exits into "One South." PRETTYWOMAN un-
screws the cable. MEAT picks up the leather and re-
sumes lacing.)

MEAT
Keeps my fingers nimble.

PRETTYWOMAN
You given this much thought? About where you'll go.
What you'll do?

MEAT
That's Bobby's job. I just want to go someplace where
the water's warm and all the fish look like they've been
painted. *(Beat)* Maybe you should play a little on that
guitar, get Trapdoor used to it.

> PRETTYWOMAN
> *(strums awkwardly)*
> **How'd he get the name Trapdoor?**

> MEAT
> **We say it 'cause it bugs him, mostly.** *(Beat)* **Supposed to be a story he was the last hangman.**

> PRETTYWOMAN
> **Him?**

> MEAT
> **Why not. All you got to do is close your eyes and pull a lever. I don't know, ask Bobby, he's been here the longest.**

> *(PRETTYWOMAN plays disjointedly.)*

> You're not very good at that, are you?

> PRETTYWOMAN
> I always wanted to learn, promised myself I would in here.

> MEAT
> You'll be José fucken Feliciano time you finish that nickel. *(Beat)* I'm gonna go see what it looks like down there.

Why did I suggest these particular cuts?

The information about the prison's construction and about Trapdoor (Mr. Witnicki, a guard who figures prominently in the play) is interesting, but it is *not compelling in the immediate circumstance of the scene in which it occurs* in this draft. Similarly, Prettywoman's expertise with cards is a belated payoff of a setup made in the play's very first scene; but it has *insufficient resonance in the play's greater scheme* to survive an edit. As for Meat's manual dexterity, we see it enacted; he doesn't need to tell us why he's doing it.

But, playwriting is not an exact science. Suggestions for revising a script are just that, *suggestions,* and Stephen Reid was free to accept or reject mine. During the two-week workshop, he noticed that when changes were discussed, he rarely made any alterations exactly as requested. Instead, he was stimulated to write "a third thing." In other words, his revisions addressed the issues raised by the actors, the director, or me, but he dealt with those issues in his own particular way.

Here, then, is the revised scene, as read at the public workshop presentation of *Doing the Book:*

(PRETTYWOMAN plays disjointedly.)

MEAT
You're not very good at that, are you?

PRETTYWOMAN
I always wanted to learn, promised myself I would in here.

MEAT
You'll be Jose fucken Feliciano time you finish that nickel. *(Beat)* I'm gonna go see if Bobby needs anything. Keep six. *(Explains:)* Watch Witnicki.

PRETTYWOMAN
Maybe I can help with the cutting.

(MEAT measures PRETTYWOMAN's bicep with a thumb and forefinger.)

MEAT
You play, we'll cut.

Another scene follows, in which Roscoe, a slimy convict who desires Prettywoman sexually, brings Bobby some drugs hidden in a hollowed-out book. This gives

Prettywoman information about Bobby he did not have before, since Bobby wants Prettywoman to give up his own drug habit. At this point, the playwright inserted the exchange between Prettywoman and Meat about whether or not Mr. Witnicki was the last hangman before Canada outlawed the death penalty.

Though I had suggested that this digression be cut, the playwright decided to retain it, making it work better for character revelation by moving it to a slightly later point in the play. The information has a greater impact in the revised version because, at the end of the scene, in a monologue delivered to the audience, Mr. Witnicki explains why he is called "Trapdoor" by the inmates. It's *not* because he was the last hangman:

WITNICKI
The name calling persists because there is a truth buried in their lie. *(Beat)* I was in the Korean War. We're not supposed to call it a war; it was officially declared a Police Action under the U.N. I was a young man, hell, I was a boy, just off a farm up near here. I was so young I had to use my brother's I.D. to enlist. I was in Korea for one week, in the summer of '53. I arrived the same day as the order for all the troops to return. I was disappointed not to see any action, so disappointed that I volunteered for a "Special Mission." I thought they were going to send us out on reconnaissance or something. *(Beat)* We hanged twenty-three of our own men that day. Aussies, Kiwis, a couple of Sikh men, some Brits, there was an American black man, I remember. He was from New Jersey. These were the men who had raped civilians, deserted their posts. *(Beat)* The black man from New Jersey had rolled a grenade into a friendly's tent because they had taken all his money in a dice game. *(Beat)* My job was to stand under the platform. It was hot that day, so hot, I remember, I had to take my shirt off. We worked all through the afternoon. *(Beat)* After they were pronounced dead by the doctor and lowered down onto my

shoulder, I would carry them. I remember how warm their skin was on my back.

Your dialogue should work for you, but it may work against you. Dialogue that stops your play's forward motion should be cut, condensed, or moved to another part of the script. Which part? Whichever part will best serve your overall purpose of informing the audience about character and action, without losing their interest. Again, this is a decision that only you can make.

3. *Are you giving the audience a lot of information too quickly?*

It used to be said that important information needs to be given three times for an audience to absorb it, which is a condescending notion; still, you can't overload an audience without risk. If you do, they may retain everything except what is crucial.

4. *Are you telling the audience what the characters in your play already know, or should know?*

My favorite example of this is the classic introduction, "Have you met my mother, the Countess?"

Be careful not to make this mistake.

5. *Are you telling the audience what to feel?*

Why? Instead, let them observe the behavior of your characters without any editorializing on your part. If that behavior interests them, they are certain to respond emotionally, though they may not all feel the same thing. Telling your audience what to feel is a clear indication that you don't fully trust the theatrical power of your dramatic story.

If the following lines, or others like them, start to appear in your dialogue, be extremely careful. You may be telling your audience what to feel without meaning to do so:

> "No matter what happens, my darling, you and I will go on together."
> "Why can't people be kinder to each other?"
> "It's not anybody's fault. It's this sick society we live in."
> "Please don't die. I couldn't bear it."
> "You won't get away with this!"
> "Those Nazis—what brutes!"

No doubt you can make up your own examples.

6. A related question to #5: *Are you leading your audience to a rational conclusion—a "moral"—before they're ready to reach it on their own?*

Contemporary audiences are quick to sense this sort of manipulation, and they tend to resist it. You know a lot more about every aspect of your play than they do, so focus on what your *characters* want, what they do, and what they say. Over the course of your play, the small interactions of human beings will create an organic dramatic vision. If you get those interactions right, intellectual conclusions and emotional connections to the characters will follow naturally.

7. *Do your characters have sufficiently individualized speech patterns?*

Can you tell one character from another by their speech patterns alone? Does the "music" of your play express what you want it to? Counterpoint, harmony, the different sounds of different instruments, and other musical strategies can be easily adapted to spoken drama, and used as structural tools for your play.

Almost any play by Sam Shepard is a good example of this musicality in drama; you might read his *Tooth of Crime* and *True West* to see how he does it. Eugene

O'Neill's *Long Day's Journey into Night* and Tennessee Williams's *A Streetcar Named Desire* are also useful examples.

8. Go over any long speeches. *Could some interruptions improve them?*

One character's response to another is a common way to keep your play moving forward, especially if the response is unpredictable, yet renews focus on the character's goal.

One useful technique has the second character not responding directly to the first, but talking about something completely different. The fact that there is no communication between two characters in the same physical space is funny, and a gifted playwright can sculpt this non-communication in such a way that the characters' separate responses make a kind of sense when heard together. Anton Chekhov does this in *Three Sisters* when, as counterpoint to a discussion taking place in the drawing room, a character enters from another room saying, "It's all nonsense, of course." This character is taking part in a conversation we have not heard, but his audible comment serves as a gloss on the conversation that we *have* witnessed.

9. Conversely, identify places where you have back-and-forth dialogue in which one character is saying standard, conventional things. *Can you eliminate the interruptions so that the first character's monologue can build effectively?*

Any long speech must grow naturally out of the preceding dialogue, and it must lead somewhere pertinent. If you can then follow this speech with either a *better* long speech by another character or a short deflating response, you will increase the audience's attention.

Here's another example from Stephen Reid's *Doing the Book:*

> PRETTYWOMAN
> How'd you get caught?

> BOBBY
> Like most bank robbers. I woke up one morning and my yard was full of Plymouths.

> PRETTYWOMAN
> Bobby, whatever become of those guys on the escape? The kid who took the hostage?

> BOBBY
> He's not around no more. Meat tell you about that? *(Pause)* About a week after they run us down to the hole, we all got sectioned. Me, the kid, and Dallas, that was my partner at the time. So I tell Dallas we had to look out for the kid, what happened wasn't right. Anyway, they used to open our three doors together for showers or whatever. So this one morning at breakfast I pass by and Tommy's still sleeping, that was the kid's name. I pick up Tommy's tray too, they used to feed us through this end barrier. I come back down the tier, a tray in each hand, and I remember lookin' in at him, thinking, where'd Tommy get a turtleneck? Then I realized he'd cut his throat. He was lying there stone fucken dead.

> PRETTYWOMAN
> That's ugly.

> BOBBY
> It gets uglier. I looked up at the barrier and both coppers are standing there waiting for a reaction. I was half asleep, so now it dawns on me one of them is the hostage guy. They must have spotted Tommy during count, left him for me to see.

> PRETTYWOMAN
> What did you do?

BOBBY
I walked to my cell, still carrying both trays, and I sat down and ate every fucken mouthful. First off of my tray, then off of Tommy's. Then I walked back up to the barrier, set the trays on the slot, and gave the guy a look, so what?

PRETTYWOMAN
What did the guard do?

BOBBY
He closed my door and never bothered me again.

PRETTYWOMAN
Your partner see, too?

BOBBY
Dallas? He bolted for his drum and tossed his cookies all over the place.

PRETTYWOMAN
Is he out now?

BOBBY
No, not long after that Dallas started not showering, or coming out at all. Then one day I went and looked in his cell. *(Pause)* I stood there and watched my best friend eating his own shit. Nowadays he's up in psych, fully sectioned and drowning in Thorazine. Every morning they dress him up in plastic handcuffs and a football helmet so he don't hurt himself when he falls down.

PRETTYWOMAN
That's a terrible and sad story.

BOBBY
It was a terrible and sad time.

What would happen, do you think, if Stephen Reid *deleted* Prettywoman's dialogue (which only seems to interrupt Bobby as he tells a story he wants to tell anyway), and *condensed* and *tightened* the resulting monologue? That option leads to another question: What event or realization provokes Bobby to revisit the horror of his discovery, and relate the story to Prettywoman? And yet another possibility: Would this story be more forceful if it were *dramatized* within the play, say as a dream sequence?

In the Cahoots workshop, we discussed these options. Here is the scene as Stephen Reid revised it; as you'll see, he addressed our concerns without abandoning the dialogue format:

PRETTYWOMAN
If you don't mind me asking, how'd you first get caught?

BOBBY
Like most bank robbers. I woke up one morning and my yard was full of Plymouths.

PRETTYWOMAN
You always got the slick answers. *(Beat)* I found out something about you while I was up in the hospital.

BOBBY
What's that?

PRETTYWOMAN
That you send canteen and bleach up to the AIDS guys.

BOBBY
So now you know my secret.

PRETTYWOMAN
I think that's a nice thing to know about somebody. I like that about prison, the way guys stick together, look out for one another. It's a bit like the Rez.

BOBBY
So you think that's noble, huh? *(Beat)* Did you meet my partner while you were up there?

PRETTYWOMAN
I thought Meat was your partner.

BOBBY
Before Meat. This was a guy down in the end cell of
the hospital? Maybe you saw him? The one they put a
football helmet and plastic handcuffs on before they take
him out for exercise, so he won't hurt himself when he
falls down.

PRETTYWOMAN
That was your partner?

BOBBY
Dallas used to be a regular, before our great escape.
(Beat) Sit down, I'm going to tell you all about *noble.*
Years ago, me and Dallas are banging together this escape play, and we get this bright idea to create a diver-
sion. So we con this kid, he wasn't all there, into taking
a hostage. But the play backfired because it put the whole
joint on special alert. When me and Dallas poked our
heads out of the tunnel, they were waiting for us. So the
kid, he hangs tough, doesn't say word one, and winds up
getting sectioned along with Dallas and me. Now, the
kicker is, about a week later, the kid gets a letter from
his parole board saying he made his ticket.

PRETTYWOMAN
You mean he had his parole? Before the hostage, and
he didn't know? Whew, some kicker.

BOBBY
It gets better. About a week after they run us all down
to the hole, I tell Dallas we had to look out for the kid.
What happened wasn't right. Anyway, they used to open
our three doors together for showers or whatever. So this
one morning at breakfast, I pass by and Tommy's still
sleeping, that was the kid's name, so I pick up Tommy's
tray too, they used to feed us through this end slot in
the barrier. I come back down the tier, a tray in each
hand, and I remember looking in at him, thinking,

where'd Tommy get a turtleneck? Then I realized he'd cut his throat. He was staring up at the ceiling, stone fucken dead.

PRETTYWOMAN
That's ugly.

BOBBY
It gets uglier. I looked back up at the barrier, and both coppers are standing there waiting for a reaction. I must've been half asleep because now it dawns on me, one of the guards is the hostage guy. They must have found Tommy dead during count, left him for me to see.

PRETTYWOMAN
What did you do?

BOBBY
I walked to my cell, still carrying both trays, and I sat down and ate every fucken mouthful. First off my tray, then off of Tommy's. Then I walked back up to the barrier, set both trays on the slot, and asked the guy what was for lunch. *(Beat)* He closed my door and never bothered me again.

PRETTYWOMAN
Your partner see any of this?

BOBBY
Dallas? He bolted for his drum and tossed his cookies. Not long after that, Dallas started not showering, or exercising, or coming out at all. Then one day, I went and looked in his cell. *(Beat)* I stood there and watched my best friend eating his own shit. *(Beat)* These days, he's up there, fully sectioned and drowning in Thorazine.

PRETTYWOMAN
That's a terrible and sad story.

BOBBY
It was a terrible and sad time.

The addition of significant detail, at the same time
as the playwright has given Bobby more of a reason
to tell the story—in order to teach Prettywoman that
prison camaraderie is not, in fact, like that of the Rez
(Indian reserve)—strengthens the scene.

10. *Do you expect your dialogue to do* all *the work of
communicating your ideas to the audience?*

In our everyday lives, we are always aware, though
often unconsciously, of other people's clothing, body language, odor, physical demeanor, and so on. We respond
to what they *say,* or don't say, but the visual, aural,
and olfactory information we're constantly assessing
definitely influences this response. So it is in the theatre. That's one of the reasons that different productions of the same play text will emphasize different
human values; it cannot be otherwise.

Playwrights who try to get every possible nuance and
meaning into their dialogue are not taking advantage
of two of the best features of the theatre: That it is
three-dimensional, and *present in real time.* Actors, designers, and technicians, coordinated by a director,
bring gifts to a playwright's work that cannot be imagined in advance. In other words, some choices made in
rehearsals can *only* be made there.

In early rehearsals, the actors will be working *backward* from your words, trying to discover what makes
their characters say something in a certain way at a
particular time. Later on, the cast will work *forward*
from the emotions and needs that they have discovered
beneath the words, articulating them in your dialogue,
and in your silences. At the same time, the décor, costumes, and lights will be created, and the visual, verbal,

and kinetic elements of the production will slowly mesh into a seamless dramatic experience. (If you're lucky!)

11. *On stage, what makes some words more powerful than others?*

At the first performance of Alfred Jarry's *Ubu Roi* in Paris in 1896, the curtain rose and a well-known actor who had been cast as Pa Ubu stepped forward to declaim the play's first word: *"Merdre!"* ("Sheeyit!") This word had never before been heard in a theatre, and it caused a riot. "Dirty" words may be commonplace in our theatres today, but there are still plenty of other words that can shock even the most sophisticated audience. Use such highly charged words only when there is a dramatic purpose to be served. Once you use them, some audiences will hear nothing else for the entire performance.

Social taboos still exist, though in an updated form, and you can learn how to use this fact to your advantage. For example, "political correctness" mandates that certain words, formerly commonplace on stage, are now not to be used. What happens if you *do* use them?

If a character you've created *really* needs to speak in a patently offensive way, allow him or her to do so. A character with racist views may use either genteel euphemisms or vicious epithets, depending on the situation. Aunt Dan in Wallace Shawn's provocative play *Aunt Dan and Lemon* is an excellent example. She is persuasive, perversely and subversively so, and some people who should have known better thought the playwright was expressing *his* views through her. The common notion that characters speak directly for playwrights, and that authors share their characters' experiences, opinions, and manners of speech, is often wrong. Still, this assumption may be a disguised compliment to a playwright's skill at making such characters seem real.

Anyone who expects characters in plays to speak and behave as if they were social role models is naïve. It's a lot more interesting, and more fun, to present characters who at first seem nasty and disgusting, then get the audience to understand them a little and accept them as human, through the play's action. You can also reverse the process: Start with characters who appear to be humane and upright, then slowly reveal them as corrupt, hypocritical thugs. You can even, if you're really good, do both at once: Read or see Henrik Ibsen's *An Enemy of the People* for a terrific example. Is the pompous and impatient Dr. Stockman, full of intellectual snobbery, better or worse than the genial, glad-handing, salt-of-the-earth Mayor?

Artistic choices have social consequences, but don't use that as an excuse to censor yourself. Imagine your "difficult" characters, and let them be fully who they are, warts and all. Remember, other characters in your play may speak and behave quite differently, and they are no less "yours."

12. *Are the silences in your play as powerful as the words?*

The power of silence in a primarily verbal medium cannot be overstressed, and many playwrights have used this power to their advantage. Study the pauses, moments and silences in the stage directions of Samuel Beckett and Harold Pinter, to see how these masters do it.

One brilliant contemporary use of both sound and silence can be found in Franz Xaver Kroetz's *Request Concert*. The protagonist of this piece is a woman who comes home from work, turns on the radio, and quietly gets ready for bed. As the music that the radio audience has asked for fills the theatre, we slowly realize that the woman before us is preparing to commit suicide. She never says a word. The counterpoint of the woman's silence with the music (which seems increasingly shallow and heartless) is shattering.

Can you think of equally effective ways to communicate theatrically without words, or by using words in unusual ways? Words and silence are not just vehicles to convey logic, emotion, and clear meaning; they are also incantations, symbols, mirrors, hammers. You must shape them with imagination, courage, and common sense to achieve your artistic goal.

13. *Where it makes sense to use jargon, are you doing so effectively?*

Characters in plays often converse using specialized vocabularies, because human beings do. Lawyers, computer programmers, educators, the military, scientists, stockbrokers, priests, football coaches, and other specialists all have their own ways of saying things, and their expertise tends to exclude those who are not in the know. This exclusion can be a blessing for a playwright, because comic possibilities abound.

In classic drama, Molière's *The Middle-Class Aristocrat* and *The Doctor In Spite of Himself* take full advantage of this fact. A good contemporary example is the specialized language created by playwright Larry Shue for his off-Broadway hit *The Foreigner.* This comedy concerns an Englishman, Charlie, whose wife has left him. Charlie is severely depressed, and his old army buddy Froggy arranges a trip to rural Georgia, where Charlie is to stay in Betty Meeks's hunting lodge. But Charlie is in no mood to socialize, so Froggy tells the widow Meeks that Charlie comes from some exotic place and speaks no English. This turns out to be a terrible strategy for Charlie, who soon finds himself overhearing both personal confidences and the local Ku Klux Klan's nefarious plans.

Rather than being left alone, as he desires, Charlie is trapped by Froggy's presentation of him as a well-known *raconteur* at home. Fascinated, Betty and her friends (who have never met a foreigner before) insist that Charlie tell them a story in his own outlandish tongue. And Charlie must invent both story and language!

After a few false starts, Charlie begins the tale of an old woman and Marla, her lovely but brainless daughter. To get the full effect of this wonderful scene, you must read the following dialogue aloud:

CHARLIE
Ah! Byootsky dottsky! Perch damasa baxa raxa. Hai.

(In a silly, youthful falsetto.)

"Mirlo *meech*no, mirlo em?" dichni Marla omsk, "y preeznia prasnia, preeznia praznia, preep?"

"Hai schmotka!" mirlotski momsk. "Per dontcha hopni skipni truda wudsk!"

"Meem? Hopni skipni truda wudsk? Ha! Ha! Ha! No! No! No!

(Aside.)

Heh! Heh! Heh!

(Aloud.)

Adios, momsk!"

(With his left hand, he imitates a skipping youth.)

Hopni, skipni, hopni, skipni, hopni, skipni truda wudsk.

(His tone becomes ominous.)

Meemskivai—omby odderzeiden der foretz, mirduschka—*Om*skivar!

(Deep, decadent, hungry voice.)

"Broizhni, broizhni! Broizhni, broizhni!"

Yach. Aglianastica, Omskivar. Das leetskicheelden ranski haidven Omski's inda vutz. "Mir-*lo*," Omski deech praznadya.

(Rubbing his stomach.)

"Miro-*lo!* Porlo papno ob*scrod*nyi! Das

(Imitating with his right hand a huge, slovenly beast crashing through the forest.)

broizhni, broizhni! Broizhni, broizhni!" Y byootsky dottsky? Hai.

(Skipping in a semi-circle with his left hand.)

"Hopni, skipni, hopni, skipni, hopni, skipni—!"

(Right hand, starting an opposite semi-circle toward the same point.)

"Broizhni, broizhni! Broizhni, broizhni—!"

(Left hand.)

"Hopni, skipni, hopni—."

(Right hand.)

"Broizhni, broizhni—."

(Left.)

"Hopni, skipni—."

(Right.)

"Broizhni—."

(The two hands confront each other.)

"Ah?"

(As Marla, in a fearless—not to say foolhardy—falsetto, chanting loudly.)

"Irlo mirlo momsky meem! Eevno peevno pomsky peem!"

(A moment—then the right hand, with a snort, gobbles the left and remains alone. CHARLIE, with a shrug, tells the moral:)

Blit?

While you may never need to invent a language for your characters to that great a degree, you will surely have to learn to use the language we share in diverse and innovative ways.

Here's a different contemporary use of jargon, again from Tom Stoppard's *Travesties*. In this scene, Carr is arguing with Cecily, a librarian, about politics. Carr is a dyed-in-the-wool reactionary, while Cecily is a fierce Marxist-Leninist who mistakenly thinks that Carr is Tristan Tzara, the Dadaist poet. Carr is very attracted to Cecily. She accuses him of fantasizing about her with her clothes off. He denies it heatedly—then Stoppard, still parodying Oscar Wilde's *The Importance of Being Earnest,* gives us the following:

> *(Faintly, from 1974, comes the sound of a big band playing "The Stripper." CARR is in a trance. The music builds. CECILY might perhaps climb on to her desk. The desk may have "cabaret lights" built into it for use at this point.)*

CECILY

The only way is the way of Marx and Lenin, the enemy of all revisionism!—of opportunist liberal economism!—of social-chauvinist bourgeois individualism!—quasi-Dadaist paternalism!—pseudo-Wildean aphorism!—sub-Joycean catechism and dogmatism! —cubism!—expressionism!—rheumatism!—

CARR

Get 'em off!
(The light snaps back to normal.)

CECILY

I don't think you ought to talk to me like that during library hours. However, as the reference section is about to close for lunch I will overlook it. Intellectual curiosity is not so common that one can afford to discourage it. What kind of books were you wanting?

CARR

Books? What books? What do you mean, Cecily, by books? I have read Mr. Lenin's article and I don't need to read any more. I have come to tell you that you seem to me to be the visible personification of absolute perfection.

CECILY

In body or mind?

CARR

In every way.

CECILY

Oh, Tristan!

> CARR

You will love me back and tell me all your secrets, won't you?

> CECILY

You silly boy! Of course! I have waited for you for months.

> CARR
> *(amazed)*

For months?

> CECILY

Ever since Jack told me he had a younger brother who was a decadent nihilist it has been my girlish dream to reform you and to love you.

> CARR

Oh, Cecily!

(Her embrace drags him down out of sight behind her desk. He resurfaces momentarily—)

But, my dear Cecily, you don't mean that you couldn't love me if—

(—and is dragged down again.)

There are as many kinds of dialogue as there are playwrights, and while it may be inspirational to look at how others have written dialogue, ultimately you will have to find your own path through a forest of options. Whether your characters speak tersely or abundantly, whether they tell the truth, or lie, or both, whether audiences will quote individual lines from your plays or simply experience an overall effect, the words you choose are extremely important.

Which leads to a final question to ask yourself:

14. *Are you trying to polish your dialogue prematurely?*

Don't. Resist the temptation to perfect everything too soon. That habit can really bog you down. Instead, get your play *written*. Like just about everything else in your play, the dialogue can be cut, focused, shifted, increased, pointed, clarified, and otherwise improved in subsequent drafts.

❖❖ 5

Comings and Goings

T HE COMINGS AND GOINGS of characters in plays are such basic elements of dramatic structure that playwrights often take them for granted. But when you understand the importance of these building blocks, when you're able to order your characters' presence and absence with maximum impact, the entrances and exits that you construct can help you create uncommonly effective theatre.

In life, when you first meet someone special, your emotions may range from delight, excitement, and curiosity, to fear and even terror. When a special person leaves your presence, you might feel anything from abandonment and loss to profound joy, or (more likely) some emotion between these extremes. Such feelings, in whatever proportion, tell you that your life either *has* changed in some crucial way because a special person is present or absent—or that it *will* change.

In writing your plays, *you* decide which characters will have that strong an effect on an audience.

Both entrances and exits are potent stage actions that either reinforce characters and keep the plot moving forward, or sabotage them. *Sabotage* them? Yes. As a playwright, you need to learn when to support your characters, and when it makes dramatic sense to undercut them.

For example, you may be writing a scene in which two of your characters are falling in love too quickly—honestly so, but prematurely for the story you want to tell. You might subvert the romance with the entrance of a third person, or an animal. You might have one of the lovers exit for some odd but human reason. This event will change the tone of the scene, permit you to delay the expression of certain emotions for a more appropriate moment in the play, and will likely increase audience interest. Juxtaposing contrasting emotions by following private moments with public ones, or the reverse, tends to do that as well, and entrances and exits are quite useful for creating or destroying dramatic intimacy.

What makes a memorable entrance or exit? Let's look at some strong examples from both classic and contemporary plays:

In *Tartuffe,* Molière keeps his title character offstage for two complete acts of a five-act play, while other characters describe Tartuffe in such contradictory ways that the audience's desire to meet the man himself is continually heightened. Act One passes—no Tartuffe. Act Two goes by—still no Tartuffe. Act Three begins. Even now, the audience doesn't *see* Tartuffe; they *hear* him tell his valet: "Hang up my hair shirt, Laurent . . ." Only then does Tartuffe come on stage. This is an entrance the audience has been waiting for, craving, demanding, so when it finally happens it's dramatically very satisfying. For over three hundred years, Molière's masterful teasing has given actors a great opportunity to make an indelible first impression. At the moment of Tartuffe's first entrance, the audience is *paying attention*.

Shakespeare's *The Winter's Tale* contains one of the most mysterious and provocative exits in dramatic literature. Antigonus speaks, then leaves the scene. Shakespeare's stage direction?

Exit, pursued by a bear.

Wow! The stakes, at least for Antigonus, couldn't get much higher; and with one bold stroke, Shakespeare has revealed a dramatic universe in which nature, both "animal" and "human," can destroy as easily as it creates.

There are many ways to stage that crucial Shakespearean moment, each as resonant as the director can make it, each revealing something about the world of the play as the director interprets it. Is *The Winter's Tale* realistic? Surrealistic? A fairy tale? A cartoon? All these possibilities, and others, can be found in Shakespeare's text.

Samuel Beckett's *Waiting for Godot* turns routine notions of entrance and exit inside out. The title character, Godot, does not appear in the play. Or, to put it another way: the *real* title character ("Waiting") is on stage during the entire performance!

Vladimir and Estragon, the two tramps who await Godot's arrival, do a variety of things to pass the time, but eventually they decide to leave. At the end of Act I, and again at the end of Act II, one says to the other, "Let's go." His companion replies, "Yes. Let's go." Now comes Beckett's exquisite stage direction: *They do not move.* Vladimir and Estragon don't exit; eventually, the *audience* does. By thus reversing the usual order of things, Beckett dramatizes both stasis and movement in such a way that we no longer take either for granted.

Here's an example of an unusual entrance, from my play *Devil on Tundra:*

(On the tundra, north of Yellowknife, Northwest Territories, Canada. It's midwinter: dark and cold, with the aurora borealis casting an eerie glow on the barrenness below. Wind whistles across the stage, and the aurora makes its own distinctive sounds. Enter SUSAN and BARRY. Dressed for the subzero weather, they still manage to argue.)

BARRY
You'll see. All your organizations, temples, churches, whatever, big fat ones like the Catholic Church or little hole-in-the-wall snake-handling sects, they'll all dry up and blow away. The earth cult is coming back, and the goddess will not be denied. It's only a matter of . . .

SUSAN
Time? Let's look at time. Four thousand years of time. Don't underestimate us. Others have. Hittites, Jebusites, Amalekites . . .

BARRY
Trilobites . . .

SUSAN
They're all history. And we're still here.

BARRY
So what? Things change. Like the small print in the mutual fund ads, "past performance is no guarantee of future" whatever. No, my earth goddess will kill your sky god, tear him to pieces, and share the dead meat with all the *real* peoples of the world.

SUSAN
Including the vegetarians?

BARRY
Don't blaspheme.

SUSAN

You are *so* full of shit.

BARRY

Susan, I love you. You're my sister. See the light. Become one of us.

SUSAN

I do see the light. Every week, I light candles.

BARRY

So do we! And my tradition's older than yours.

SUSAN

I'm your sister, remember? My tradition *is* your tradition. This goddess kick is a yuppie fad.

(A glass-enclosed shower stall rises out of the ground. Inside it, surrounded by clouds of steam, is KEVIN. He is soaping himself.)

—Barry . . . ?

KEVIN
(Singing, to the tune of "Louise")
Ev'ry little breeze seems to whisper disease,
Birds in the trees seem to twitter disease,
Ya da da daaa, ya da da daaa, I love you, disease.

(Rinsing off, and changing his tune)
Holes in the ozone
Holes in your head
Holes in your wallet
You're better off dead.

(KEVIN snaps his fingers. A towel appears. It says "I'm a little devil" and has a picture of a grinning traditional devil with a tail, horns, and pitchfork. Humming, KEVIN dries his hair, then notices the towel design. Irritated, he snaps his fingers again. Another towel appears. This one says "Holiday Inn.")

—Much better.

BARRY

Yeah?

SUSAN

What's *that?*

BARRY

What?

SUSAN

Him. The naked guy.

BARRY

Naked guy? Where?

KEVIN

Well, I'll be damned.

Your purpose in bringing *any* character onstage is *to raise the stakes*—by moving the play forward, by complicating the action, or by increasing suspense. The first time an audience meets a character, they feel the pleasure of discovery. When this feeling is accompanied by surprise, audience pleasure increases. Initial appearances of a familiar character type, or subsequent appearances of an individualized character they've already met, give an audience opportunities for recognition.

Whatever your chosen subject, if you can find ways to combine all three qualities—joy, surprise, recognition—in each entrance, your audience will be ready and willing to focus on your characters, to watch and listen to them, expecting them to exhibit meaningful interactive behavior, expressive speech, powerful silence, and either important change or a dramatically valid *inability* to change.

But *when* should you bring a new character on, or bring an old character back?

There's no formula, but here are a few (far from exhaustive) guidelines:

1. *Introduce a character when the audience needs to learn some important information that is unknown to at least one other person on stage.*

This "information" might be a plot complication, or the sudden simplifying of an earlier complication. However, if the information that the audience needs to know *is* the entering character, you have an even better reason for introducing that person at that precise moment. In *Devil on Tundra*, Kevin is such a character, and the circumstances of his entrance are so strange that audience attention is immediately focused on him.

2. *Introduce a character when you want to change the play's level of energy.*

In theatre, energy is often tied to expectation; when a character enters, the audience automatically expects something to change. But *what* will change? Will there be conflict, or unexpected harmony? Will the dramatic issue at the heart of the play be posed in a new and exciting form? This last question is important for speeding up the forward motion in your play. Adding a combative new character just before the end of an act, for instance, can immediately increase interest in what's going to happen in the *next* act. This is especially useful to convince an audience to return after intermission, which is not something a playwright can take for granted.

3. *Bring on a character when you need to show the third side of a dramatic triangle.*

It doesn't matter whether it's a triangle of love, rivalry, revenge, or anything else. The old saying, "two's company, three's a crowd," suggests that three characters offer many more dramatic possibilities than do two characters. An odd number of characters tends to be more provocative than an even number, because the imbalance is inherently unstable—and therefore full of theatrical potential.

The following excerpt comes from my play *Prayers,* which is set in a monastery during Henry VIII's persecution of the Catholic Church in England. Toss, a mute juggler, has sought refuge near a statue of the Virgin Mary. Two monks, William and Hugh, discuss whether or not to take the ragged stranger in:

WILLIAM
On your way then, lad. May Jesus and his holy mother protect you.

HUGH
Father William, hold. You spoke of Christian charity . . .

WILLIAM
Ay?

HUGH
'Twill soon be dark. Let our guest take refuge here, and escape with us at daybreak.

WILLIAM
What if the army attack us in the night?

HUGH
Then his soul goes to God with two clerics for company, and ours with our last earthly deed one of charity.

WILLIAM
Then—will you stay with us, lad?

(TOSS nods yes.)

WILLIAM
'Tis settled.—Well done, Hugh! I thank thee for a good rebuke and a good example.—Stranger, may God be with us all this night.—Come, Brother. Let's finish our little chores.

(The MONKS leave. TOSS tries to sleep, but he can't. He's restless. The crucifix and the statue still spook him. Finally, he takes the chalice, the bread basket and one candlestick, and starts to juggle them. As he warms up, his juggling gets more and more complicated and adept. He's transported. BROTHER HUGH comes back. When he sees what TOSS is doing, he explodes.)

HUGH
I knew it! Sacrilege! Blasphemer!

(BROTHER HUGH grabs a lighted torch from a sconce and goes after the terrified TOSS, who's trapped between HUGH and the statue of the Virgin. Suddenly, the statue speaks!)

MIRIAM
Hughie . . . Hughie . . . It's not nice to play with fire.

HUGH
O holy Virgin! O miracle! O sainted mother of our dear Lord, come to life to punish the transgressor! O—

MIRIAM
Oh, shut up.

(MIRIAM gestures. BROTHER HUGH turns to stone and sinks into the floor. The torch flies back into its sconce. MIRIAM smiles at TOSS.)

—So what's new?

(TOSS faints dead away. MIRIAM checks out her breath.)

—Is it me?

This momentary "triangle" is somewhat unusual, but the principle—and the power it can give you—should be clear.

4. *Bring on a new character when you need a "mediator" between the audience and an "extreme" character who is already on the stage.*

This is useful when you've created a character who is *unlike* your audience, one whom the audience fears or finds emotionally incomprehensible. In such a case, audiences tend to withdraw their attention. You don't want to lose them, yet you certainly don't want to limit your repertoire of characters only to those with whom your audiences will feel comfortable. Contrasting an "extreme" character with a "safe" (or at least safer) character helps reassure an audience that they are still in a familiar and manageable dramatic universe.

The entrance of a new character, one with whom the audience can feel an emotional kinship, helps you reinforce the audience's sense of security. This security results, in turn, in increased attention to your play. Here's an example:

(Lights come up on A MAN standing center stage. He has dark hair, with a lock brushed over one eye, a toothbrush mustache, and he wears lederhosen *and a Tyrolean hat. The MAN looks at the audience—and suddenly throws a fit. Screaming incomprehensibly, he jumps up and down on the furniture, climbs the walls, rolls around on the floor, foams at the mouth. Enter A WOMAN. She is blonde, average, housewifey.)*

WOMAN
Adolf? Adolf, what are you doing?

(He stops abruptly.)

                         MAN
    Oh—just thinking.

The above is my recollection of the opening moments
of a script about Adolf Hitler and Eva Braun that I
read many years ago. I remember neither the play's
title nor its author, but I'll never forget the scene's
admirable economy and wit. As a dramatic character,
Hitler is simultaneously fascinating, repellent, and
dangerous. Most audiences will respond defensively the
moment they see him.

The audience's way into the scene—and out of their
defensiveness—is provided by Eva Braun, who inno-
cently yet adroitly asks the very question we want answered. At that moment, we're utterly focused on what's
happening. Hitler's reply is both funny and scary, because we recognize both its deep psychological truth
and, at the same moment, its unexpected payoff of a
clever and somewhat threatening theatrical setup.

Well, then, what of exits?

They're a little harder.

Whereas entrances offer discovery, surprise, and recognition, exits remind us of the passage of time, the
conclusion of action, a separate (and invisible) offstage
reality to which a departing character is presumably
going. Moreover, if the entrance of a character is a
symbolic birth, then an exit is a symbolic death. As
with any other death, our response may be sadness,
happiness, tension, relief of tension, or any combination thereof.

Because exits so often conclude actions an audience
has witnessed, and because exits give that audience its
last sight of now-familiar characters, a sense of loss or
abandonment is not uncommon when characters leave

the stage. However, if a character's exit contains the seeds of his or her return, we have another way to keep an audience involved. Audiences captivated by a character they want to see more of tend to stay in their seats.

If your playwriting includes implicit or explicit references to the universe outside the theatre (e.g., the mention of current or past "real world" events and personalities, familiar place names, or household products), characters' exits can provide an audience with some very resonant moments. By giving your invented character, whom the audience now knows through the play's action, a "real world" destination, task, or goal, you play on the difference between imagination and experience, between art and memory. This can lead the audience to that "willing suspension of disbelief" that helps make your characters and their actions credible both emotionally and intellectually.

If you keep in mind that every entrance is an exit *from* some unseen offstage reality, and every exit an entrance *to* some unseen offstage reality, you will automatically strengthen your characters' motives for appearing in the action you're dramatizing. In other words, characters exit, and characters enter, *for a reason*. Is it their reason, or yours? Of course, it's yours; you are the playwright. But the more it *appears* to be theirs, the more persuasive your dramatic world will be.

Ask yourself, when characters are to enter or exit, what do they *want?* Where are they coming from? Where are they going? Is the stage world their goal, or is the stage merely a transitional space between two unseen and unknowable offstage realities?

Here's a tip: Write a few of the "offstage scenes," those that take place only in your mind, scenes an audience will probably never see. Doing this will help you keep track of your characters while they are offstage and will help you find out exactly when *they* need to come back on stage, to the "real" action of the play. You may even discover that your offstage scene is so lively that you'll bring it onstage in some form.

You can also play with dramatic conventions so deep-rooted that people hardly realize they *are* conventions. For example, characters in plays rarely leave the stage to go to the bathroom, although we certainly do so in our daily lives. Comic possibilities? Tragic possibilities? Explore and find out.

Another technique, to be used sparingly: Have a character leave a scene very soon after it has begun, not for the sake of the technique, to be sure, but for the sake of suspense, mystery, variety and forward motion. That character needs a strong agenda. The audience does not need to know what the agenda is; just that the character has one. They will automatically expect to see that character again. This is an example of an obvious setup, one that needs to be paid off in a clever way on the character's return.

If an entrance or an exit feels misplaced or just wrong, it probably is. Remember, entrances and exits are both causes and results of dramatic action. What feels completely off in one draft may be perfectly right in the next, so experiment freely with structural changes.

How should characters enter or exit?

Doors are the customary choice, although the theatre will accommodate just about any imaginable way of making the transition. I've enjoyed plays in which characters came in or left through windows, through walls, down or up a chimney, even (as in *Devil on Tundra*) into or out of the ground. *Anything* on any stage can be an entrance, or an exit. It depends what the play requires, and how imaginative you are in fulfilling those requirements.

Whether you're creating an imaginary world on stage or recreating an everyday world based on our commonly observed reality, you'll use entrances and exits. It's best to order them consciously to express your dramatic vision as clearly as you can.

❖❖ 6

If (When) You Get Stuck

YOU'VE WRITTEN:

ACT ONE
Scene 1

You've written more than that. And then, for some reason, you've stopped dead. You're stuck, frozen, unable to write another line of your play, and all sorts of nasty things (including panic) are going through your mind. What to do?

Robert Anderson, author of *Tea and Sympathy* and other plays, has a sign over his desk that reads, "Nobody *asked* you to be a playwright." This reminder helps keep him from self-pity, from casting himself as a victim. He chose his profession, and he chooses it again, actively, every working day.

Nothing is as patient as a blank sheet of paper or computer screen; nothing is as impatient as a frustrated playwright. Learning artistic patience is crucial. We have all heard this common view:

To be an artist, you must write every day, at the same time of day, in the same place, for a set period of time, or complete a set number of pages at every writing session.

92

That's sensible advice, as far as it goes, and certainly if you can be that regular about your playwriting, then doubtless it will be productive.

But if you listened to *sensible* advice, you might not be a playwright at all.

You may be one of those playwrights who, for whatever reason, cannot write every day. Are your moods more mercurial, your life less regular, your output less predictable than you would wish? Do you sit down intending to work, but instead find yourself daydreaming, balancing your checkbook, surfing the Internet, reading a detective novel, or doing anything rather than write? Perhaps, at other times, you write for hours on end, oblivious to family, friends, and all the temptations of a non-artistic life. Perhaps you fear that you don't have the will and discipline that a "real" playwright needs, that though you like *being a playwright,* you find it really difficult actually to *write plays.* Possibly you use your urge to write plays—and your failure to do so consistently—as evidence that you're unfit for art, if not for life.

Maybe you are saying nothing because you have nothing to say.

Or maybe that's your fear—not your reality.

Don't let anything stop you.

Negative thinking and self-deprecation are common among aspiring artists in any genre. How can you get over these obstacles, and develop a productive writing attitude that will help you get those scripts down on paper?

"All-or-nothing" thinking is a major adversary. "If I don't write every day, I'm a hypocrite, so I won't allow myself to write, period. Better a 'wannabe' than a fraud," is an example of such thinking. The same principle can be applied to writing for less time, or completing fewer pages, than you have planned. Whatever you do—even if it's to stare at a blank sheet of paper or computer screen for a couple of hours without writing a word—try to think of it all as creative work. The playwriting mind is complicated, and your creative rhythms may not be those that you wish you had, or that other people necessarily understand.

By the same token, don't lie to yourself. Creativity flows best when some sort of routine has been set up, and writing a play solely in your head does not make it available for production.

Don't spend too much time trying to get everything perfect, or making your play "actor-proof," or attempting to forestall every possible objection to your script. Analysis can lead to paralysis. If you sense your own self-criticism slowing you down, tell that insidious voice to *shut up*.

Some playwrights prepare for a writing session by exercising, stretching for flexibility and walking or running in order to get oxygen-rich blood to the brain. Others drink strong coffee or listen to music. Whatever your particular warm-up regime, it's right for you *if it works*. If it doesn't work, try something else. Use whatever you need to get started.

In writing plays, momentum may be more important than complete clarity about what you are doing. This is especially true of first drafts. So, once you've started writing, keep going. Recognize as a snare and a delusion the temptation to answer a ringing telephone, or to see if any royalty checks have come in the mail.

It's not that simple, of course. You will need to take breaks every once in a while, and life does tend to intervene now and then, just because it's life. But by deciding to write plays, you have traded simplicity and leisure for primeval chaos. As a creator, it's your job to bring order out of that chaos. Inevitably, this requires effort, and a plan tailored to your own particular needs.

Some writers need a deadline in order to write. This is a problem, because most plays are written on "spec," and there is no externally imposed deadline involved. The script submission deadlines of new play contests can be helpful, and you should try to use them to prod yourself into finishing your play. The downside of this is that you may submit scripts prematurely, before they are really ready to be considered for production.

Daydreaming time is important to a playwright. When you daydream, you follow to their artistic conclusions all the "what-ifs?" you have asked yourself. But try to balance the daydreaming with note-taking, then reread the notes when you need to ground yourself in the reality of *work done*.

Research is important, too. Whether you are writing a play set in an unfamiliar time and place, or your play needs authentic details of a particular business or profession, or you need scientific information, doing the requisite research can help you feel ready to get back to the keyboard. Yes, there is a downside: You may spend more time researching than writing. Worse, your research can overwhelm your play. Knowing when to *quit* researching, knowing when to *alter facts* for dramatic purposes, knowing, finally, when to get on with the script, are things best learned on the job.

Some playwrights draft their scripts in longhand, in exercise books or on looseleaf paper. Typewriters are still a tool of choice for many, though most playwrights now probably use computers. If you do use a computer, any of the standard word-processing programs work just fine. There is scriptwriting software available, but it is less useful for writing plays than for television and film scripts.

Use any method that works; you can even mix and match them from one draft to the next. But the search for just the "right" tools should not impede your writing. Spending time and money on hardware and software is the contemporary equivalent of sharpening a dozen pencils and putting them all in a row before writing a word.

Identify any resistance you have to writing, but don't make too much of it. Keep it in its proper place, seeing it as a minor annoyance, not a major roadblock. Keep a notebook handy for ideas, lines, potential projects that come to mind. You may never use any of these items, but jotting them down helps keep your mind sharp and ready for writing.

Some writers get their best insights at unexpected times, in unlikely places (the shower is a wonderful place for sudden visions of how to solve a playwriting problem). Dreams may provide you with characters, symbols, bits of dialogue, even whole scenes.

I have said that you should write a first draft straight through, stopping as infrequently as possible. But there is *another* way of drafting a play that is not quite so singleminded, yet may be more suitable for you. Some playwrights rewrite the opening scenes of a play several times before moving on to the next section, trying things out, adding or discarding *beats* (units of action), characters, bits and pieces of dialogue until they are comfortable with what is already on the page. It's not the most efficient way to craft a play, but it may not make much sense to speak of efficiency when it comes to creating a stage event from scratch. The only test is, does it help you get the play written?

When you are up against a playwriting obstacle that seems immovable, take a walk. Take a drive. Take a nap. This may seem like abandoning the struggle, but don't put too much stock in confrontational strategies unless they work for you. Instead, pose the difficulty to your unconscious mind, then let it go. Sleep on it. It's amazing how often a solution will present itself when you wake up.

What if you *really* get stuck?

Humorist Robert Benchley was once advised: "Sit down at your desk, scroll a page into your typewriter, type 'The' and something wonderful will surely follow." Benchley tried it. He stared at his "The" for a long time, then typed "hell with it," put on his hat and left for the nearest tavern.

The point of that anecdote, for our purposes, is that within a few days, Benchley was writing again.

Dry spells are part of the game, and you will get through them best if you don't panic. There are a thousand little tricks that a playwright can use to get past a chasm of uninspiration or inertia.

Here's an exercise that I've found helpful: I have a canvas bag filled with small slips of paper, each with the name of an object written on it. When I get stuck and can't seem to get going, I draw out one of the paper slips and write a monologue from the object's point of view.

What words have I written on the little slips? *Washcloth. Pork chop. Candle. Champagne flute. Running shoe. Condom. Tooth. Stethoscope. Bassoon. Cigar. Basketball. Floppy disk. Pocket watch. Penny. Wok. Wedding ring. Leash. Emerald. Toilet bowl. Venus flytrap. Bowling pin. Rolling pin. Jockstrap. Bible.* And so on.

Here's a monologue created with this exercise:

PORK CHOP
"Milk-fed, low-fat, the *other* white meat." Phooey! Damn yuppie pigletoids and pigletettes screwin' up a

great gruntin', squealin' industry an' way of life! Whadda they say? "Bring home the bacon!" They don't say, "Bring home the lettuce an' tomato." They don't say, "Bring home some pale, pallid, scrawny, limp piece a *nouvelle cuisine.*" Naw! They want *pork!* And good ol' God-fearin' Baptist pork is what I am. See this? Thick an' juicy? This is pig fat! From a big, fat, dead, corn-fed Iowa hog. Fry me up in a pan and listen when the good Christian folk smell that sizzle. What'll they say? "Lard have mercy!" Lard. That's a joke, son. Tryin' ta pretty me up. What for? I got my uses in this world, I ain't just another pukey piece a tofu in the sky. First, food. You eat me, you know you've et. Greasy hands, greasy face, satisfaction. Second, symbol. Without me, the yids an' the ragheads couldn't sin so easy. They'd hafta be swallowin' some other kinda Satan just ta feel human. Jews call me *trayf.* Forbidden food. Unclean, they say. But tasteeee? Oooh! Seen 'em in Chinese restaurants, the chosen people, choosin' the good stuff. Laws, schmaws, they know how to eat. Marinate me, baby. Stroke a little a that there barbecue sauce on me, fire up the coals and let me do my thing. I can make ya drool without half tryin', an' I got the odor a sanctity beat by a country mile . . .

Here's another:

JOCKSTRAP

That's "athletic supporter" to you, madam, if you don't mind. There are those who use the vulgar term, but that is scarcely a habit into which one should get, as the bishop said to the nun. Sorry? Oh. No offense meant, madam, I assure you. Where was I? Yes. I am, I know, a figure of fun, a phlegm-faced schoolboy's idea of humor, but I am proof against all such denigration. I have upheld the mighty in my day, bringing protection and solace to heroes of the gridiron, cradling in my embrace the future of kings. What care I for the calumny of the ignorant? I live in a warm place, I eat the rarest of cheeses when I choose, I consort with princes and privates alike. I am in good odor with the mighty. What care I that the loathsome Marx Bros., not content with their own juvenile japery, sought to "send up" that lovely young actress in that rightly-forgotten touring play by replacing the crown jewels in the casket with me? Ah, the moment when she gazed on me, never expecting the honor. Ah, the struggle to contain her laughter as she covered it with dismay, dismay at learning that the crown jewels had been stolen from the casket and taken God knows where? What a trouper she was! And I, coiled like a snake in that casket, chagrined at being put to such ignominious use, how she sensed my torment and forgave me, forgave me, and here my tale must end, madam, what next occurred is not for ears as shell-like as your own . . .

These flights of fancy have no purpose in themselves, but are merely means to an end. So far, these monologues have never failed me as a way of getting past a bad case of writer's block. I relax, I laugh, then I go back to my play.

Work habits, like subject matter and style, are highly personal. Even if the ideal of writing several pages every day cannot be reached, the quest need not be abandoned, nor even postponed. Start now. Do *what* you can *when* you can. Then do a little more.

Ready?

ACT ONE
Scene 2

and so on.

❖❖ 7

Finding Your Style

P ROFESSIONAL SCRIPT READERS often say that they are
looking for "unique voices," and that's a telling
phrase. Distinctive plays stand out primarily because
they *sound* different. Structure is influential, too; but
structures tend to change in the process of revision far
more than does a play's "voice." In fact, playwrights
revise the structure of their plays *so that* audiences can
hear the play's voice more clearly. Style and voice are
not exactly the same thing. *Style* is an attribute of a
play, while *voice* is generally thought of as an attribute
of the playwright. Since the playwright creates the play,
the two concepts are closely linked.

How can you make your play's voice *and* its structure
so distinctive that your style will instantly impress
anyone who reads or sees your play?

You may already have this great gift as a playwright,
or you may need to develop it as you master your craft.
One way to stimulate your stylistic imagination is to
read the plays I mention (all are published in either
trade or acting editions—see the Appendix), to see for
yourself how effective diverse playwriting styles can be.

Colleagues and mentors

As a working playwright, you can look on every other playwright, from Sophocles to Shakespeare to Shaw to Ntozake Shange, as your colleagues—and mentors—in a very demanding field. Learn from them, borrow techniques from them, but don't forget to make their techniques your own. It's in the transformation, not the borrowing, that your own style will become unique, and your "voice" will be heard.

One way to develop a distinctive style is by creating dramatic parallels between your new play and an older work—a play, a poem, a book, a film—that functions as an inspiration, an influence, or as an object of homage or parody. For example, there's a famous moment in the movie *Now, Voyager:* Paul Henried lights two cigarettes at once, then offers one of them to Bette Davis, who accepts it. It's an elegant metaphor for seduction. But in adapting this idea, Christopher Durang's comedy *A History of the American Film* achieves its style through parody: Two cigarettes are lighted, one is offered—but the young woman responds, "I don't smoke."

This moment, so effective and sophisticated in the movie, immediately looks foolish. Durang deftly skewers both the pretentiousness of *Now, Voyager* and the Freudian innuendo of the society that gave it birth. Part of the moment's effectiveness in the play comes from its comic simplicity, and part from the comparison between the film and Durang's play. It helps to have seen the movie (probably on television, the great hidden influence on Durang's play), but the scene would be funny in any case.

Other strategies don't depend on earlier works of other writers. Let's look at a very different playwriting style, that of Ntozake Shange. This playwright calls her much-produced and controversial theatre piece *for colored girls who have considered suicide / when the rainbow is enuf* a "choreopoem." While not a play in the traditional sense, it is a powerful stage work. Its mood shifts frequently, one emotion gliding into another, in a way that is stimulating for performers and audiences alike. Its softness and jagged edges, its bitterness and belly laughs, reverberate in ways that conventional theatre rarely achieves.

Any playwright can learn a lot from *for colored girls . . .* , especially from its presentation of character and its reliance on vignettes for structure instead of the customary long arc of dramatic experience. This "short story" structure places a lot of emphasis on the acting ensemble, in which the characters are referred to as "Lady in Green," "Lady in Blue," and so on. Their stories, hilarious and harrowing by turns, never lose their individual clarity, and yet a sense of community, a community under siege from inside and outside itself, is unmistakable. As a result, the play has a style that immediately lifts it out of the ordinary:

LADY IN BLUE
a friend is hard to press charges against

LADY IN RED
if you know him
you must have wanted it

LADY IN PURPLE
a misunderstanding

LADY IN RED
you know
these things happen

LADY IN BLUE
are you sure
you didnt suggest

LADY IN PURPLE
had you been drinkin

LADY IN RED
a rapist is always to be a stranger
to be legitimate
someone you never saw
a man wit obvious problems

LADY IN PURPLE
pin-ups attached to the insides of his lapels

LADY IN BLUE
ticket stubs from porno flicks in his pocket

LADY IN PURPLE
a lil dick

LADY IN RED
or a strong mother

LADY IN BLUE
or just a brutal virgin

LADY IN RED
but if you've been seen in public wit him
danced one dance
kissed him good-bye lightly

LADY IN PURPLE
wit closed mouth

LADY IN BLUE
pressin charges will be as hard
as keepin yr legs closed
while five fools try to run a train on you

LADY IN RED
these men friends of ours
who smile nice
stay employed
and take us out to dinner

LADY IN PURPLE
lock the door behind you

LADY IN BLUE
wit fist in face
to fuck

LADY IN RED
who make elaborate mediterranean dinners
& let the art ensemble carry all ethical burdens
while they invite a coupla friends over to have you
are sufferin from latent rapist bravado
& we are left wit the scars

LADY IN BLUE
bein betrayed by men who know us

LADY IN PURPLE
& expect
like the stranger
we always thot waz comin

LADY IN BLUE
that we will submit

LADY IN PURPLE
we must have known

LADY IN RED
women relinquish all personal rights
in the presence of a man
who apparently cd be considered a rapist

LADY IN PURPLE
especially if he has been considered a friend

LADY IN BLUE
& is no less worthy of bein beat within an inch of his life
bein publicly ridiculed
havin two fists shoved up his ass

LADY IN RED
than the stranger
we always thot it wd be

LADY IN BLUE
who never showed up

LADY IN RED
cuz it turns out the nature of rape has changed

LADY IN BLUE
we can now meet them in circles we frequent for
companionship

LADY IN PURPLE
we see them at the coffeehouse

LADY IN BLUE
wit someone else we know

LADY IN RED
we cd even have em over for dinner
& get raped in our own houses
by invitation
a friend

*The lights change, and the ladies are all hit
by an imaginary slap . . .*

The sense of betrayal caused by date rape is given a
powerful collective voice here, and poetic style becomes
dramatic substance.

One of the best and least expected shifts of tone in
a play can be found in Shakespeare's *Romeo and Juliet*.
The two teenagers are having their first private conver-

sation. Though their families are bitter enemies, Romeo and Juliet are strongly attracted to each other. They have declared their love in a fairly conventional way, but suddenly the play takes a realistic turn:

ROMEO
Lady, by yonder blessèd moon I vow,
That tips with silver all these fruit-tree tops,—

JULIET
O, swear not by the moon, the inconstant moon,
That monthly changes in her circled orb,
Lest that thy love prove likewise variable.

ROMEO
What shall I swear by?

JULIET
Do not swear at all;
Or, if thou wilt, swear by thy gracious self,
Which is the god of my idolatry,
And I'll believe thee.

ROMEO
If my heart's dear love—

JULIET
Well, do not swear . . .

This sort of quick tonal shift in a context of standard conventions—such as a declaration of first love—is a hallmark of Shakespeare's style, and it's one effective way to move a play forward and at the same time deepen its character revelation. This passage is our first intimation that Juliet, though younger than Romeo, is somewhat wiser and more mature than he. Instinctively, she dismisses a romantic cliché by taking it seriously, and insisting that Romeo do the same, sets him a challenge far more impressive than any conventional coy denial of her feelings would be. Her frank vulnerability is both realistic and endearing. Romeo's response to her honesty is likewise honest, in his own terms. Their temperaments are different, yet complementary. This shift in tone raises the play's stakes in an important way; the coming tragedy doesn't just happen to two generic youngsters, it happens to two distinct human beings for whom the audience has come to care strongly.

Another example of style creating dramatic substance is found in Maria Irene Fornés's short play *A Vietnamese Wedding,* which imagines a village wedding in Vietnam, with members of the audience being asked by the narrator to play various family roles. Could anything be more charming or innocuous? Don't believe it: At the height of the Vietnam War, this subversive little piece did as much to evoke my personal sense of horror at the loss of life and the decimation of culture in Southeast Asia as anything on television or in the press.

No doubt *A Vietnamese Wedding* would have a different effect now, but it is very much worth reading for its unusual dramatic strategy, its indirectness, and its sly power. Any time a play starts out seeming quaint and ends up being visceral, other playwrights can learn from it.

Work plays

One playwriting genre in which style emerges from situation is the "work play." In this genre, whatever the major characters in a play are up to, there is always physical work of some kind being done—sometimes in the foreground, sometimes in the background. The relationship between this "work" and the characters' "play" can be significant, with the "work" serving as both context and as a metaphor for any number of things. Complex texture is a feature of every persuasive work play's style.

Tina Howe's *The Art of Dining* is a good example. By showing the contrast between the frazzled kitchen and the elegant dining room of a tiny, fashionable New Jersey restaurant, by having actual meals prepared and served during the action, the play grounds itself in a visible, credible reality. There's no problem with authenticity here; the audience can literally *smell* wonderful aromas emanating from the working kitchen on stage. The play celebrates a variety of appetites, and food becomes a simultaneous comic metaphor for sensual, sexual, intellectual, and emotional exchange.

Imagine this scene: Ellen, the restaurant's co-owner, is in the kitchen preparing entrées. Her husband Cal, also a co-owner, travels back and forth between the kitchen and the dining area as both host and waiter. There are three occupied tables in the dining area. At the first are Paul and Hannah, a married couple; at the second, Elizabeth, a shy writer, and her prospective publisher, David; at the third are three women friends, Herrick, Nessa, and Tony.

CAL
(pouring wine for HERRICK)
Puligny Montrachet.

ELLEN
(fussing over her entrées)
Ooooooohhhhmmmmm . . .

HERRICK
(tasting the wine)
Mmmmmmmmmmmmm . . .

ELLEN
(inhaling the fragrance)
Aaaaaaaaahhhhhhh!

HERRICK
(crooning over her wine in a different register)
Uuuuuuuuuuhhh!

NESSA
(eagerly, to HERRICK)
How is it?

HANNAH
Oh, Paul, that was . . .

ELLEN
Arrange the peach slices on the duck . . .

HERRICK
Symphonic!

HANNAH
. . . . . divine!

DAVID
(to ELIZABETH)
That . . . was an outstanding soup!

ELLEN
(gazing at the veal)
. . . . beautiful!

PAUL
Better than the Pavillon, better than the Tour d'Argent . . .

CAL
(pouring wine for NESSA)
Mademoiselle . . .

TONY
I can hardly wait.

ELIZABETH
I wasn't sure how to get here . . .

ELLEN
. . . ladle the Mornay on the veal . . .

NESSA
(tastes her wine and makes little mewing sounds)

HANNAH
. . . better than *any* meal I've had anywhere . . .

ELLEN
(handling the duck)
. . . inspired!

PAUL
Here, here . . .

TONY
(grabs NESSA's hand)
I'm going to have a heart attack!

ELLEN
(fussing over the bass)
Yes, my little bass . . .

PAUL
The best . . . !

TONY
(her hand on her heart)
No, really, I am!

HANNAH
Well, Ken and Diva did rave, remember?

NESSA
(to TONY)
Just don't keel over until the food comes!

DAVID
In fact, *both* soups were outstanding!

ELLEN
(inhaling the bass)

Devastating . . .

ELIZABETH
(to DAVID)

I almost got on the wrong bus.

HERRICK
(raises her glass to her friends)

To the meal!

NESSA

To the meal!

TONY

To the meal!

CAL
(dives back into the kitchen, to ELLEN)

They can hardly wait!

ELLEN
(has put the final touches on her entrées)

All set . . .

CAL
(hoists the tray over his head)

So far . . . so good . . . *(and plunges back into the dining room)*

ELLEN
(as he disappears)

So far . . . so good.

This scene is the lead-in to a wonderfully manic section in which the women's orders get mixed up, and there are underlying conflicts about who wants what someone else has, who diets and who doesn't. You can see from the above passage how a symphonic texture for a play can be created in a working environment such as a restaurant—and how the rhythms of cooking and serving and the rhythms of the various conversations function together.

Work plays have been set in such venues as suicide prevention centers, locker rooms, factories, and the post office, to name only a few. There are obvious advantages in having the rhythms of labor serve as a structural element in a play; the audience sees activity with which it is familiar, while the playwright can motivate numerous types of action that are immediately believable within the given context.

Even if your script is not a work play *per se,* you can get quite a lot of mileage out of having at least one work *scene* in it. Whether it's George Bernard Shaw's John Tanner tinkering with an actual touring car in *Man and Superman,* or Bertolt Brecht's Anna Fierling plucking a real chicken in *Mother Courage,* the sight of a stage character performing a "real world" task (often with a prop that is seen infrequently on stage) is usually quite credible to an audience.

However you choose to create appropriate moods for your play, the texture you wish the audience to perceive, and suitable resonances for your action, your play's style is very much under your control. You may not get these elements exactly right until you are fairly far along in the process of writing and revising your script, but don't get discouraged if your style emerges slowly.

In creating your style, don't hold back. Go farther than you intended to. Take risks. Some can be calculated in advance, while others will surprise you.

❖❖ 8

Rewriting

H OW WILL YOU KNOW when the first draft of your
script is finished?

First, remember that your script does not need to be
perfect. When you have told your dramatic tale in a
form that feels relatively complete, and when you cannot write another word, *stop writing*.

Take a break.

Put the script away. This is *not* the time to evaluate
what you have written, still less to change it. So do
something else. Go to the gym for a long and well-
earned workout, then see a movie. Go to a beach, a bar,
a zoo; drift around a good museum and replenish your
image bank. The possibilities are endless.

The intensity of the project, its emotional importance
to you, any deadlines imposed by a commission contract
or by a producer, your health, your need to earn a living,
your will power, even the weather—all are factors that
will determine how long your break should be.

There are two major principles to follow:

1. *Don't go back to your script too soon.*
2. *Don't let too much time go by before you tackle
it again.*

What do such vague terms as "too soon" and "too much time" mean for you? You will figure them out through experience. Respect your instincts, and don't be discouraged. Enjoy your break; you've earned it!

When you do go back to your script and reread it, you may either love it or hate it. Either reaction means that you have picked it up too soon. Put it aside until tomorrow.

Now: Sit down and read your script aloud, *straight through*. Make sure you do so without interruption. Mark places where you wish to make changes, but don't make them yet. Keep going. Play all the characters, and read your stage directions aloud as well—in a less dramatic tone, of course:

How do you learn how and when to revise your work?

Over time, you'll develop your own strategy, but here are some questions that should get you started. Let's begin with *character* revision:

● Do all your characters sound the same?

● Do they sound different from each other in a theatrically meaningful way?

● Do you have to take a breath in the middle of a line of dialogue in order to finish it?

● Do the words make sense *to the characters who are saying them?*

● Are you repeating yourself? If so, is it for some valid purpose?

● Can you visualize what the characters are doing as they speak?

● Can you visualize what other characters on stage are doing during these speeches?

● Can you imagine what they are *thinking?*

You have written words that are meant ultimately to be spoken aloud on stage by and to other human beings, so as you listen to yourself read your script, you are casting yourself as the audience. Any questions that this first reading raises for you will likely be raised by real audiences.

Keep two things in mind: One, this first reading really ought to be *out loud*. The "theatre in your head" is too small—and it has bad acoustics. You will learn things from how your text sounds that you cannot learn any other way. Two, any questions that this reading raises do *not* have to be answered immediately. You may wish to leave some of them as questions, because it is sometimes just as valid to tantalize an audience as it is to provide them with answers. Often more so.

Read the script aloud *again*. Mark places where more changes need to be made.

Now, go back and look at the places you marked, and make the changes. Some will be cuts; some may clarify material that is too cryptic or obscure. These kinds of changes are relatively easy to make, while others—major structural revisions—are harder. For example, you may discover that a character of whom you are quite fond isn't really necessary to the plot, and that you could easily combine him or her with another character. Do so. Be merciless—but save whatever lines you cut. You can often recycle characters, events, and speeches and use them in other parts of this play or a future one.

It may now be clear that a character needs to be altered radically—that his or her gender, age, intelligence, or sensitivity is less appropriate in its present form than in some different form. This kind of revision creates more work than you think it will, because such changes alter not only the character in question, but also his or her relationships with everyone else in the play. It will be time-consuming to follow through on the results of major character changes, but it's time well spent.

And then there's *structural* revision.

How many acts does your play have? Two? Three? More? For many years, the standard non-musical play had three acts; then two acts became the standard. Lately, the three-act play seems to be coming back. You may choose whatever you think will work best for the play; there is no central authority to decide matters of aesthetics! The number of acts should relate to your play's overall structure. It may make sense, for example, to put act breaks where much time passes between scenes, if the play's rhythm allows this. As a rule, any changes you make in characters and dialogue will force changes in structure as well. The reverse is also true.

In reviewing your script, you may find that the order of scenes needs to be shuffled, or even that scenes in one act would work better (with appropriate changes) in another act. Some side-by-side scenes may have the same emotional dynamics, and would feel repetitive to an audience even if the actual content is different. Can you combine them? Or, alternatively, can you change the emotional dynamics of the second scene sufficiently from the first so as to diminish the repetitive effect?

This part of the process should improve the play's *arc*. What you usually aim for is a play that starts at one point in space and time and ends in another, with the connection between the two points made by a curve or zigzag rather than a straight line: Curves and zigzags are more complex (and therefore more interesting) both mathematically and emotionally than straight lines. But all this talk of arcs and curves is somewhat abstract. More simply: In your revision, you must try to make sure that the particular logic of your play is most forcefully expressed by the structure you have chosen.

This is not easy, because there are many structures possible for any play. How, then, do you choose among them? You may have to try several different structural arrangements before you settle on the "best." Some questions to ask yourself:

1. Does your play flow smoothly? *Do you want it to?*
2. Is the play's action predictable or surprising? *Surprise is usually good.*
3. Are the surprises reasonable, or arbitrary? *Sometimes "reasonable" is better (but not always).*
4. Is your play merely the illustration of a theme, an attitude, or a platitude, or is it a complex set of actions with multiple meanings? *The latter is harder to write, but more human — and appealing to an audience.*
5. Are there any gaps between scenes? Try adding to them, to see whether the play needs a whole scene, or just an extra "beat" here and there to scenes that already exist. *It's better to underwrite than overwrite.*
6. Are there any superfluous scenes? *Delete them.*
7. Does the play still retain its mystery for you? *If not, something's wrong either structurally or conceptually.*
8. Is the play's rhythm effective without being obvious? *Subtlety is powerful.*
9. Have you explored the full dramatic potential of your story line? *Of course not. Do so in the next draft, and the next, and so on . . .*

What if there are problems that you can't figure out how to solve?

Be patient.

One old theatre saw that often still holds true is this: *If your second act exhibits a loss of energy or flagging invention, the problem you must solve is not in Act II but in Act I!* This is a variation on the "setup/payoff" theme. It suggests that your first act must have in it the seeds of all succeeding action, so that when your play reaches a dramatic climax in the second act, it is satisfying without necessarily revealing its origin. Revising Act I to improve Act II, or even Act III, is "the art that conceals art."

That is why, in revision, you will sometimes be working backward from *effect* to *cause,* and then forward again from *cause* to *effect.* You may have to rearrange the order of any part of the script, from single lines to entire acts; and no one but you should ever know the complexity of the surgery.

Be prepared, even in revision, not to be fully conscious of what you are doing. You have written only one complete draft so far, and many of the solutions that first occur to you will bring new problems with them. You will have to deal with these in subsequent drafts. This may be upsetting, but it's quite normal.

Finally, accept the fact that playwriting is ultimately an imprecise art. Here is a long scene from *Bella Donna,* my play-in-process. Based loosely on *Lucrèce Borgia,* a play that Victor Hugo wrote in 1833, *Bella Donna* contains a number of choices, few of which are either inevitable or irrevocable. The play is set in Italy, in the early sixteenth century, but its language and some of its attitudes are deliberately contemporary:

Scene Five

(Dark stage. Projection:

Ferrara. A little later.

*Lights up on the throne room. A table with a crystal tray,
bearing a gold flagon, a silver flagon and enamel cups.
ALFONSO plays with a toy cannon. ANGELA is putting
a black patch over the eye of a larger-than-life-size golden
head of Pope Julius II.)*

ANGELA

Alfonso? Which is better? The left eye? Or the right?

ALFONSO

Both.

ANGELA

Be serious.

ALFONSO

When Julius finds out I've looted his statue from the
cathedral and melted it down for a cannon, things will
be quite serious enough.

ANGELA

Don't melt his head yet. I have plans.

ALFONSO

Playing pirate is a game for boys.

ANGELA

So is playing with toy cannons.

*(ALFONSO puts the little cannon on the floor, strikes
a match and lights the fuse. A tremendous roar; smoke
and flame. Offstage, a window breaks. ANGELA
crosses herself.)*

ANGELA

Jesus!

ALFONSO

Jesus has nothing to do with it. I've ordered several
hundred big brothers of this "toy" from the Austrian

foundries. Delivery next month. After that, the Pope can attack any time he likes. He'll lose half his army the first day.

ANGELA
Don't forget the people of Ferrara. If they think they're going to die, they'll remember their souls, and desert you.

ALFONSO
But *only* if they think they're going to die. As long as they can make money and fill their bellies, we'll be in power.

ANGELA
I think you like being the anti-Christ.

ALFONSO
I think *you* like it more.

LUCREZIA
(off)
Alfonso! *Alfonso!*

ANGELA
Here she comes.

ALFONSO
Go home, Angela.

ANGELA
Can't I stay and watch?

ALFONSO
Get!

(Giggling, ANGELA blows him a kiss and disappears through a hidden exit. ALFONSO composes himself. LU-CREZIA rushes in, agitated.)

LUCREZIA
Alfonso! Someone just vandalized my name on the palace gate. In broad daylight.

ALFONSO
Vandalized your name? Explain.

LUCREZIA
Go see for yourself. Stand among the unwashed of
Ferrara and listen to them snicker.

ALFONSO
Thank you, no.

LUCREZIA
It's treason!

ALFONSO
Come, sweetheart, sit down. We'll have some wine.

LUCREZIA
I don't want wine. I want justice.

ALFONSO
We're excommunicated. It might be wiser to ask for
mercy.

LUCREZIA
Don't patronize me.

ALFONSO
Patronize you? That's good Christian doctrine.

LUCREZIA
Stay inert, then. I'll find the guilty swine myself and
give him what he deserves.

ALFONSO
Calm down.

LUCREZIA
No! *You* get angry!

ALFONSO
What for?

LUCREZIA
What *for?*

ALFONSO
The culprit is already under arrest.

LUCREZIA
Already—! You *devil.* You're way ahead of me.

ALFONSO
This time.

LUCREZIA
Who is this person?

ALFONSO
Nobody *I* know.

LUCREZIA
Where is he?

ALFONSO
Next door. I'm about to interrogate him. Care to join me?

LUCREZIA
Alfonso: swear to me that the man will not leave here alive.

ALFONSO
If that's what you want.

LUCREZIA
Swear!

ALFONSO
Lucrezia, you have my word of honor. He dies today.—Bring the prisoner in!

(GIOVANNI is pushed in, roughly, by unseen hands. He is manacled, and his feet are chained. He has been

badly beaten. LUCREZIA reacts, then controls herself and sits on her throne.)

ALFONSO
(to GIOVANNI)
Come here. Who are you?

GIOVANNI
Don Alfonso: my name is Giovanni.

ALFONSO
Giovanni what?

GIOVANNI
Just Giovanni. I don't know my family name. I am a captain in the personal guard of His Holiness the Pope.

ALFONSO
You serve in the most elite unit in Italy, yet you don't know your name or family?

GIOVANNI
No, your grace. I assume I'm illegitimate.

ALFONSO
There are no illegitimate children, just illegitimate parents. And they are more common than you might think. Even our belovèd spouse Donna Lucrezia Borgia d'Este, here beside us, was a—love child. Did you know that?

GIOVANNI
All Europe knows it, your grace.—No offense meant, madonna.

ALFONSO
And none taken, I'm sure.

LUCREZIA
Get on with it.

ALFONSO
How did you manage to get into the Pope's guard without a pedigree?

GIOVANNI
I made my own pedigree. The Holy Father knows a warrior when he sees one.

ALFONSO
That he does. Go on.

GIOVANNI
Five years ago, I was a fisherman, the only child of Stefano and Anna Rossi. We had to fish every day just to survive. There was a big storm. Our boat capsized. Stefano and Anna couldn't swim. I tried to save them . . . Their bodies washed up on the beach. After the funeral, Father Giuseppe told me that Stefano and Anna Rossi weren't my parents. I wasn't Giovanni Rossi. There *was* no Giovanni Rossi. I was just a nameless baby in a basket abandoned at the church door. So I left my village. I learned to fight. I learned to read. I learned the world.

ALFONSO
With no clue at all to your identity?

GIOVANNI
None. Well, one. When they found me, I was wrapped in this peculiar cloth. It was long and hand-knitted, but clumsy, as though someone had tried to make a scarf but really had their mind on something else, you know? It was very colorful. Red and green and blue, shot through with gold thread in a zigzag pattern.

(LUCREZIA has risen from her throne.)

LUCREZIA
Where is that scarf now?

GIOVANNI

Oh, it's long gone. My father used it to patch a hole in the sail, and when the boat sank . . .

(LUCREZIA sits back down.)

ALFONSO

Captain, this morning, a person or persons unknown defaced the Borgia family crest. Do you know anything about this crime?

GIOVANNI

I do, your grace.

ALFONSO

What do you know?

GIOVANNI

I committed it.

ALFONSO

I see. I won't ask *why* you did so. Given your rather disconcerting candor, I fear that you would tell me.

GIOVANNI

Don Alfonso, I expressly waive any rights that I may have under Cardinal Benedetto's diplomatic immunity. Donna Lucrezia, I am sorry for what I did. It was dishonorable. I accept whatever punishment you decide is appropriate.

ALFONSO

Punishment. Ah.

LUCREZIA

Don Alfonso, I must speak with you. In private.

ALFONSO

Captain, would you please excuse us for a moment?

(GIOVANNI bows and goes out, dignified despite the chains.)

                    LUCREZIA
Alfonso—

                    ALFONSO
Nice lad. I almost hate to kill him.

                    LUCREZIA
No—

                    ALFONSO
But I gave you my word, so that's that.

                    LUCREZIA
Alfonso—

                    ALFONSO
Are you worried that my kind nature will get the better
of me? Don't be.

                    LUCREZIA
Alfonso, don't kill that boy.

                    ALFONSO
Excuse me?

                    LUCREZIA
I don't want him to die. Not just yet.

                    ALFONSO
Now or later, what's the difference?

                    LUCREZIA
Right now, sparing his life will impress the Pope.

                    ALFONSO
Right now, killing him will impress the Pope even
more. Besides, I gave you my word of honor.

                    LUCREZIA
I release you from it.

ALFONSO

You can't do that.

LUCREZIA

If I'm willing to pardon this Giovanni—is that his
name?—what difference does it make to you? *I'm* the one
he offended.

ALFONSO

Just so. He offended you. That is unpardonable.

LUCREZIA

If we should seek mercy rather than justice, we should
grant it, too.

ALFONSO

Dear Lucrezia.

LUCREZIA

Snuffing out a puny little Vatican mercenary—why
bother? Let's just exile him from Ferrara for life.

ALFONSO

The lion and his lioness don't get upset over a fleabite.

LUCREZIA

Exactly! Thank you, Alfonso.

ALFONSO

Thank me after his funeral.

LUCREZIA

His—

ALFONSO

I have given my word. Captain Giovanni must die.

LUCREZIA

Spare his life. Just until Benedetto leaves for Rome.
Then I'll take care of him myself.

ALFONSO

Can't do it.

LUCREZIA

Of course you can!

ALFONSO

Won't do it.

LUCREZIA

Whyever not?

ALFONSO

Because Giovanni No Name is your lover.

(Pause. LUCREZIA laughs.)

LUCREZIA

That's ridiculous. He just defaced my name in public!

ALFONSO

Lovers quarrel.

LUCREZIA

Oh, Alfonso, they've even got *you* believing the lies.
That hurts.

ALFONSO

Come off it, Lucrezia. I was *there*. I saw you panting
after him like a weasel in heat. I watched you exchange
masks and drag him into the Vatican. And I've had
enough of this shame and disgrace and betrayal!

LUCREZIA

Oh, have you? You hypocrite! Have you also had
enough of that insect Angela?

ALFONSO

That's different.

LUCREZIA

How?

ALFONSO
I'm a man.

LUCREZIA
In some ways.

ALFONSO
Shut up.

LUCREZIA
Alfonso—"for better and for worse." I said that on our wedding day. I say it again, now, and I mean it.

ALFONSO
Sure you do. Without me, your throat would be cut in a minute.

LUCREZIA
Without me, *your* throat would have been cut years ago.

ALFONSO
Speculation.

LUCREZIA
When you married me, you got a fortune for a dowry, the cities of Spoleto and Rimini to pay you tribute, an alliance with Rome and the protection of the Borgia family. I made you the most powerful duke in Europe.

ALFONSO
And I made *you* respectable. At least I tried.

LUCREZIA
Well, aren't you the martyr! But look at you now. Bankrupt. Excommunicated. Facing an invasion and civil war. Milking your adolescent cow. My father's dead, and you still don't have the guts to throw me to the wolves. Why not? Go ahead! Pawn my jewelry, buy more cannon, invade Rome, depose the Pope, rule the world! While Angela rules you.

ALFONSO

You Borgias. Any one of you would gag a maggot. Your
brother Cesare, with his face turned into Swiss cheese
by syphilis. Your other brothers, connivers not worth a
chicken's fart. Your mother Vannozza, the Vatican whore
who fucked and sucked her way into a fortune in real
estate while she littered Rome with her nasty bastards.
And last but not least, your father Rodrigo. The Pope
with a harem! Bribing here, backstabbing there, throw-
ing honest men into dungeons and elevating corrupt jack-
als to the college of cardinals. So rotten inside when he
died that he blew up like a pig's bladder on a stick. First
his devoted servants ransacked his bedroom looking for
money, then they broke his arms and legs so they could
squeeze his fat belly into a coffin. And God, the *stench!*
It was his putrid soul on its way to hell.

LUCREZIA

I loved him.

ALFONSO

So I've heard. Now listen: I want Giovanni to die. But
let's be fair. You may choose the *way* he dies.—Cat got
your tongue? All right. I'll just tell the guard to cut his
throat.

LUCREZIA

Stop!

ALFONSO

Or you can pour him a refreshing cup of wine.

LUCREZIA

Alfonso, that's what I planned to do all along. Only in
my own good time, when he's least expecting it.

ALFONSO

Now suits me better. Give me your hand. Where's your
wedding ring? Ah, here it is. Beautiful as ever. Lift up
the stone, and there's that old secret compartment. Look!
What a coincidence! It's full of some exotic pharmaceuti-

cal. We'll just open the gold flagon, like so, and pour in some good old Borgia magic.—All done.—Outside there: send in the prisoner!

(GIOVANNI returns.)

ALFONSO
Captain Giovanni: hear your fate. Donna Lucrezia pardons you. Therefore, *I* pardon you. God forbid that we should deprive Christendom of a faithful sword in a faithful hand.

(ALFONSO unshackles GIOVANNI.)

GIOVANNI
Clemency. I didn't expect this. I—

ALFONSO
We're not such monsters. Are we, dearest?—Tell us, what exactly are your duties in Rome?

GIOVANNI
I command a company of fifty lancers.

ALFONSO
Fifty lancers! Excellent. May I ask you a personal question?

GIOVANNI
I would be honored.

ALFONSO
What sort of salary does the Pope pay you?

GIOVANNI
The Holy Father gives me two thousand ducats a year. Out of that, I pay, feed and clothe my men and myself. Bonuses and salvage are extra, of course.

ALFONSO
Naturally. Now: suppose we offer you five thousand ducats a year.

GIOVANNI

Five thousand!

ALFONSO

Will you join our service?

GIOVANNI

I'm sorry, your grace, but . . .

ALFONSO

Once this annoying excommunication is lifted, of course.

GIOVANNI

That's not it. I have taken a sacred oath to serve the Holy Father for the next three years.

ALFONSO

A man who honors a contract. I like that. May we offer you some wine?

GIOVANNI

Don Alfonso, this morning I disgraced my uniform. This afternoon, from you and Donna Lucrezia, I am learning what Christian forgiveness is. I will gladly drink with you.

ALFONSO

Splendid.

(ALFONSO pours a drink from the silver flagon into an enamel cup. He hands another cup to LUCREZIA.)

ALFONSO

Donna Lucrezia, to show our respect for this loyal servant of the Supreme Pontiff, will you please pour?

(LUCREZIA tries to take the silver flagon.)

ALFONSO

No, dear. Only the best of wine for the best of men.

(Shaking, LUCREZIA pours GIOVANNI a cup of wine from the gold flagon.)

GIOVANNI
You do me honor. I thank you both.

ALFONSO
Our pleasure. May you be in love until the moment you die.

GIOVANNI
Don Alfonso, that's the best toast I've ever heard. The same to you and—and Donna Lucrezia.

(GIOVANNI and ALFONSO touch cups and sip with ritualistic delicacy.)

GIOVANNI
This wine is fantastic!

ALFONSO
It's a very special vintage. Captain, I regret I cannot stay and chat. Affairs of state. You understand.

GIOVANNI
I hope you and the Holy Father can resolve your differences.

ALFONSO
I'm an optimist. Farewell, Captain.

GIOVANNI
Your grace.

ALFONSO
(to LUCREZIA)
Stay with him. Share your lover's last few moments of life. You might even have time for a final tryst, if you skip the foreplay.

(ALFONSO leaves.)

GIOVANNI

Donna Lucrezia, I—

LUCREZIA

Giovanni! You just drank poison!

GIOVANNI

Poison? God, I should have suspected. You poured the wine!

LUCREZIA

Alfonso knows we were lovers. He gave me a choice: watch a guard cut your throat, or give you—

GIOVANNI
(interrupting)

Poison. And you chose.

LUCREZIA

If your throat's cut, you die; but there's an antidote to the Borgia poison. I'm the only one who knows of it. Here.

(LUCREZIA tries to touch a vial to GIOVANNI's lips. He recoils.)

GIOVANNI

Not so fast.

LUCREZIA

What's wrong?

GIOVANNI

How do I know that *that* isn't poison?

LUCREZIA

Giovanni, I'm trying to save your life!

GIOVANNI

Why?

LUCREZIA

Because—There's no time to argue. Drink this.

GIOVANNI

No! The Duke is an honorable man. You are—well, we
both know what you are. In Rome I spat in your face.
Right here in Ferrara I've turned your name into a public
joke. "Save my life." Sure.

LUCREZIA

Do you want to die? Soon even the antidote won't save
you. For the love of God, drink it now! *Drink it now!*

(Pause.)

GIOVANNI

You drink it.

LUCREZIA

What?—*Yes!*

GIOVANNI

First the poisoned wine. Lots of it!

(LUCREZIA drinks greedily from the gold flagon.)

GIOVANNI

Now this so-called antidote.

*(LUCREZIA sucks some from the vial. They wait in
silence.)*

LUCREZIA

Satisfied?

GIOVANNI

Not yet.

LUCREZIA

Giovanni—!

GIOVANNI

Read any good books lately?

LUCREZIA

For the love of God!

GIOVANNI

What do you care whether I live or die?

LUCREZIA

I have ... reasons. Your story about the scarf ...
touched me.

GIOVANNI

Touched you? Why?

LUCREZIA

Giovanni, I am Lucrezia Borgia. Am I the woman you
thought Lucrezia Borgia was?

GIOVANNI

No. No, you're—

LUCREZIA

Then take the antidote. Right now. *I beg you.*

(*A moment. She looks into his eyes. Mesmerized, he
touches his mouth to the vial.*)

LUCREZIA

Saved!—Keep that vial with you always. You never
know when you'll need it. Take this passageway. It leads
to the bedroom of my husband's mistress. Then leave
Ferrara and never come back.

GIOVANNI

You have some dark plot in hand. I wish I could figure
it out.

LUCREZIA

Plot? I just saved your miserable life! "Thank you,
Lucrezia." "You're welcome, Giovanni."—Now get out of
my palace.

(GIOVANNI hesitates, then kisses LUCREZIA with a passion that shakes them both. He leaves. LUCREZIA pours a cup of poisoned wine from the gold flagon. She seems about to drink it, but changes her mind. She toasts the absent GIOVANNI, then looks up to heaven.)

LUCREZIA

He's alive. Perotto, he's *alive*. Our son. Maybe. And my lover. Oh, *God!*

(LUCREZIA pours the poisoned wine on ALFONSO's throne. Its cushions hiss and smoke. LUCREZIA laughs wildly.

A moment. Blackout. End of Scene 5.)

My challenges in the above scene, which concludes Act I, include *raising the dramatic stakes; bringing together a number of plot strands; having the play's three main characters meet; creating one or two setups for plot twists later in the play;* and *giving the audience a strong incentive to return for Act II.*

These challenges are interrelated. Let's consider them one by one.

It is always good to "raise the dramatic stakes" when you can, but doing so in the *final scene of your first act* (of a play in two acts) is especially rewarding. This helps the audience look forward to Act II. You can also raise the stakes in the *next-to-last scene of the entire play.* Introducing a plot twist there can be useful, because by the time that scene is reached, the attentive audience member can usually see where the play is headed. An unexpected development can reinvigorate an audience's curiosity. The *final* scene of the play can then be used to tie up any loose ends, and finish the play on a note of fulfillment.

Whatever your chosen dramatic subject, structure, or style, you should seek ways to sharpen the conflicts among characters, increase the public resonance of private actions, involve your audience more intensely in the play's events, and so on. In *Bella Donna,* a giddy one-night stand between Lucrezia and Giovanni has unforeseen yet crucial consequences, which the above scene dramatizes.

Lucrezia learns that her condemnation of an unknown criminal has played right into Alfonso's hands. She has inadvertently sentenced her lover—who may also be her son!—to death. She also learns that Alfonso knows more of her activities than she thought he did. She seems thoroughly trapped, but as the scene unfolds, she works her way out of what at first looked like an impossible situation. This automatically raises the dramatic stakes, because we want to see how and whether Lucrezia will continue to outwit her powerful and equally clever husband.

Having the play's three main characters finally meet—in a crisis situation—also brings together several strands of the plot. Independently of each other, both Lucrezia and Alfonso have schemed successfully to get Giovanni from Rome to Ferrara, and so he is part of Cardinal Benedetto's delegation. This means that anything that happens to Giovanni personally will also affect the political and religious situation of the play, namely the Pope's excommunication of Alfonso, Lucrezia, and the duchy of Ferrara. On a more immediate level, it's just plain shivery fun to watch Alfonso toy with both Lucrezia and Giovanni.

Giovanni's naïveté contrasts with the manipulative expertise of both Alfonso and Lucrezia; but at the crisis point, Lucrezia is forced to appeal to Giovanni's instinctive trust in people. This trust has just been betrayed by Alfonso! We and Lucrezia know this, but Giovanni isn't convinced. At that moment, his fate is out of Lucrezia's hands. All her power turns into anxiety. What will Giovanni do? *And who is he?*

That question, in turn, sets up the potential for significant plot developments in Act Two. Will Alfonso learn that Giovanni may be Lucrezia's son? Will Giovanni learn this? How will each react? In addition, the fact that Lucrezia has saved Giovanni's life will have obvious consequences for her relationship with Alfonso. The ongoing power struggle between husband and wife will get even richer. What will happen next?

The easiest and most obvious way for the audience to find that out is to return after the intermission.

I have rewritten the poisoning scene many times, including and excluding various pieces of information. I had a head start, as there is a somewhat similar scene in Hugo's play; but my scene is longer and emotionally more complex.

I began with a straight translation of Victor Hugo's play *Lucrèce Borgia,* then deleted a number of characters who turned out to be extraneous to the central story. In this particular scene, I eliminated most of the pomp and ritual that Hugo was able to associate with the court of Alfonso d'Este, Duke of Ferrara. Hugo's play has more than 25 characters, because the economics of the French theatre of 1833 encouraged him to create roles for that many actors. My play has five characters. It's a smaller canvas. Is there some loss here? Of course. But there is a gain as well. My play is tighter and more focused, and that is worth something.

Throughout all the revisions, the "spine" of the scene has remained the same: Giovanni is poisoned and Lucrezia must save him with her secret antidote. Other elements, such as the presence of Angela at the beginning of the scene, the cannon made from the statue of Pope Julius II, and the brief political discussion, have been added detail by detail during the process of revision. I also extended and deepened Alfonso's vicious manipulation of both Lucrezia and Giovanni.

Are my choices the best *possible* choices? For me, yes. For another playwright with a different dramatic agenda, they might not be. That's what I mean about playwriting being an imprecise business.

I stated earlier that the play's language and vision are deliberately contemporary. In other words, I am not trying to replicate the *actual* story of Lucrezia Borgia, the politics of 15th-century Rome and Ferrara, or the kind of quasi-Shakespearean language we often associate with drama set centuries ago. While these are all of interest, they are not pertinent, *because I, the playwright, have taken from history only what is useful for this particular play.* I have freely mixed fact and fiction, and the language reflects this.

I am unable to write in 15th-century Italian, and even if I had that capacity, it would only irritate a modern English-speaking audience to no good purpose. So, I use the language of my own place and time as creatively as I can. This is, after all, what Shakespeare did in his plays set in earlier times. His characters speak stage versions of Elizabethan English, not Julius Caesar's actual Latin, Othello's Venetian, or Macbeth's medieval Scottish. In other words, Shakespeare has substituted his vision of his own world for the "reality" of his settings of time and place, and we have come to accept his vision because it is cogent and persuasive. In his own day, of course, he was using contemporary stage language, *not* the language of the period in which the plays are set.

If Shakespeare can do this, so can the rest of us.

You are free to recreate other times and places in your own way, without worrying about getting all the "real" details right. Sometimes it makes sense to acknowledge this. In the *Bella Donna* manuscript, I have written the following:

> This play was inspired by historical events and personalities, but it makes no claim to historical accuracy. It's not a documentary. Whatever realism it contains is imaginative rather than literal. Its multiple settings are meant to be created swiftly, deftly, preferably using light and sound rather than the sort of décor that takes time and stagehands to shift. And yet, the effect should be sumptuous.

Such a note may help lessen the fears of prospective producers that the play requires expensive costumes and cumbersome sets. In fact, such things would diminish the play.

I haven't forgotten that you just finished your first draft. You still have many decisions to make. You may wish to do another draft of your script immediately, or you may want to hear your play read by others, even in its current rough state, *before* you begin to revise. This is a delicate judgment, because your private playwriting is now at the beginning of its journey toward a public life that is, after all, its ultimate goal.

What is your play ready for? What are *you* ready for?

❖❖ 9

Hearing Your Play

YOU HAVE TO HEAR YOUR PLAY.
You can only imagine up to a point what it will sound like, and you must get past that point to revise it effectively. This is a difficult moment for a playwright, because now you will have to involve other people in your creative process. But there is no other way. In the theatre, audiences respond to what they hear as well as to what they see, what they interpret, and what they imagine. So, you need to know what they will hear, how they will react, and whether or not your play is saying what you want it to say, in the way you want it said.

Cold readings
If you know any professional actors, by all means invite those who could play the roles you've written to meet together for a *cold reading*. "Cold" simply means "unrehearsed."

Also ask someone to read the stage directions aloud. Don't do this yourself.

Get copies of your script to the actors a few days before the reading, and invite them to ask you (privately) any questions they may have that will help them approach their characters effectively. Then, at the reading, sit back and listen carefully to the actors as they read your words.

If you don't know any professional actors, ask non-professionals. Sometimes so-called amateur actors (from a community theatre group, for example) have skills that may surprise you. Or simply ask friends to read your play to you. Try to choose friends whose ability to read aloud from an unfamiliar text is sufficient to be helpful to you.

You can learn quite a bit from hearing your play read with some imagination and verve. Your readers' instincts may not be as acute as those of professionals, their training may be non-existent, and their choices of intonation, emphasis, and delivery may tend toward stereotype. Even so, they can reveal a lot about what work you still have to do on your script.

Even acting "choices" made by professionals can be wrong, but as it's your play, you can always stop the reading, explain what you want, and start again. However, you should consider listening to "wrong" approaches to the script, and their consequences, because you may learn from those readings how to adjust the script in a way that will diminish such errors.

This first reading is a useful experience, because you have lots of influence but very little control over what happens. Your preparation for production has begun. You will hear your play come alive in ways you never expected, and you will probably also become aware of "dead" moments that will upset you. Passages you thought were brilliant can turn out to be overwritten and self-conscious, while what you thought was routine, as you wrote, may be surprisingly powerful, affecting, or funny—sometimes all three.

Some playwrights invite family and friends to serve as audience for this first reading; others will not share a new script with *anyone* until they have written several more drafts. There are compelling arguments for either approach, and you will discover by experience which option works better for you. Family and friends may not give you the critical feedback you need to improve your play, but their support can do wonders for your need to keep going. Just don't confuse their commentary with objective evaluation.

Experienced actors, whether amateur or professional, are wonderful resources for a playwright. Many of them love to work on brand-new material, and their comments and questions can be extremely helpful. Of course, some quite talented actors are not very good at cold readings; they need time and rehearsal to perform effectively. Others give great first readings, because they have the ability to make quick character choices. Such actors are perfect for your rewriting needs, though they may not be as suitable for an actual *production* unless they can also deepen and sustain their characterizations. Different needs require different skills.

There are three ways to test a play in a reading:

One is the reading of the script itself, during which you can listen to how it sounds. Take notes! Don't be too concerned if an actor goes off on what seems to you a wrong tangent; after all, this reading is unrehearsed for a reason. Mark the moment. Revisit it later to see if the verbal cues—the words, their rhythm, the breathing spaces, etc.—that you have given the actor have anything to do with the actor's wrong choices. Is it possible that your cues can be misinterpreted in ways that don't enrich the experience? Similarly, where an actor makes exactly the choice you intended, don't assume that your work is therefore done. Be wary: Your cues and the actor's responses may be completely in sync, but this might also be sheer, unrepeatable coincidence.

Second, watch your audience (which includes you). At what points in the play are they paying close attention? When do they seem to be drifting away? Do they shift and cough? Do they laugh where you want them to? Do you ever find *yourself* distant from your own writing? This sort of reaction will help you get the rhythms and the revelations of your play right; it is indispensable.

Third, pay attention to any discussion of the script that occurs after the reading, whether it is between you and the actors, or you and any audience you have invited. Playwrights differ in their assessment of the usefulness of such discussions. Obviously, the more theatrically savvy your audience, the more helpful they can be. *But be careful: Your creative process depends heavily on your unconscious mind.* If what is unconscious becomes conscious prematurely, it may have a negative impact on your rewriting. So there's a risk involved in listening to post-reading comments. They are usually meant to be helpful, and may actually be so, if they are made at the right moment. Unfortunately, it is no easy matter to know when that moment has arrived.

Playwright Romulus Linney (*Why The Lord Came to Sand Mountain*, etc.) once observed, "There are three basic human drives: food, sex, and the urge to rewrite someone else's play." Most people don't really want to rewrite your play; they want *you* to rewrite it to suit them. You may or may not wish to do this.

Ask those who comment on your play to tell you which characters and incidents interested them, which confused them, where they felt drawn into the play, where they felt distant from it, and where they felt the play was either over- or underwritten. Get them to tell you about anything they think is problematic in the script, *but ask them not to offer unsolicited solutions.*

Solutions are your business alone. You are the playwright, and it's your play. You may not agree that a "problem" really *is* a problem, or that it needs to be solved at this stage of your play's development. Listen closely to any questions the actors ask, and find out where they kept reading, and where they noticed obstacles.

Many playwrights prefer not to answer questions. Instead, they write both questions and comments down for a more leisurely reflection in private. This practice helps eliminate the natural defensiveness that any artist feels when his or her work-in-progress is criticized, and allows the dramatist to focus on the content of such scrutiny, rather than its source, its tone, or his or her reaction to it.

You are under no obligation to please anyone but yourself.

If you keep that in mind, you will be less defensive, more able to find merit in the comments of others, when merit exists. You, the playwright, are more important than the audience, and your play is more important than you are.

No one likes to be criticized, but wise playwrights learn to find the real value in informed, objective commentary on their work. Whether you get good criticism from a professional dramaturg, from your best friend, or from Uncle Moe is irrelevant. By "good" criticism I do not mean mere praise, although it is nice to have someone recognize all the effort you've put in.

Rather, I mean respectful but incisive comments on your work that take seriously both your effort and your achievement *so far.* Finding this kind of criticism is not easy. The theatre is notorious for encouraging a level of critical discussion that zigzags from sentimental mush, to hyperbole, to character assassination. That sort of commentary has little value in helping you get your script right. Good criticism may make you uncomfortable. It may raise issues that you would rather not deal with, and it should not be confused with cheerleading, nurturance, or the reinforcement of your self-esteem. It is for adults.

Probably, though, since you have just finished a first draft, *you* are the best critic of your own work—if you allow yourself to be. Be slow and sensible in your revisions. Sometimes, though people commenting on a new play describe the play that *they* would write, not the play that *you* have written or want to write, their comments may help you clarify your own views. At this early stage of your play's development, you know more about it than anyone—even though you don't know everything that you will know later on.

Playwriting groups

Another way to "hear your play" is to join a good playwriting group. This is not for every playwright, nor can every playwright who could benefit from such a group find a suitable one. Wherever you happen to live, though, you should look into the possibilities.

Among the factors that make such groups useful is the presence of eight to twelve dramatists of roughly comparable gifts (but different artistic visions), who agree on a common protocol by which to support each other's creative process. They meet every week, or every other week, for several hours, during which time they read aloud scenes from each other's current work.

Reading scenes from a play-in-process rather than complete acts or plays means that a playwright can hear his or her work when it is freshest, and when the writer has not invested so much time and energy in completing a script that he or she resists considering possible revisions. The group's primary purposes are to provide a structure for the presentation of smaller, less polished dramatic units, and to provide each member playwright with a supportive artistic community that does not permit nasty, destructive criticism on the one hand, or cozy, useless praise on the other.

These groups work best when its members also have some talent and previous experience at cold readings of other playwrights' scripts. Some groups also have actors and directors as members, and certainly the questions and comments that such artists offer can be of great value. But the primary response comes from one's peers. Depending on their ability and the honesty of their criticism, their comments can really help you shape a play *in the way you want to shape it*.

Guidelines that have proven helpful to running such groups successfully:

• *Facilitating sessions and scheduling readers should be rotated among the group's members.*

• *No interruptions are permitted during the reading of a scene or fragment, unless the playwright whose work it is feels the need to stop the reading.*

• *Following a reading, each member of the group may comment in turn, without interruption.*

• *Group members may not offer unsolicited sugges-tions on how scenes, characters, action, or dialogue should be rewritten. They may, however, report their aesthetic and emotional responses to what they heard.* Examples: "I think you should make the heroine more likable," or "You have to bring that character on much earlier in the scene," are not as useful as "I found myself losing interest during that character's monologue," or "I don't think you've fully explored the comic potential of the situation." One of the most useful comments I ever got was, "That scene needs more rock 'n' roll." The commentator didn't suggest *how* I should go about adding this missing ingredient; she trusted me to figure it out.

• *The playwright whose work is being discussed should take notes of what is said. After everyone has spoken, he or she may ask questions to clarify the others' commentary, but may not argue with the comments, or deride anyone's response.*

• *The purpose of these and any other guidelines for a playwriting group is to help each member playwright feel secure enough to take artistic risks, and to create imaginative and satisfying plays in whatever genre he or she cares to work.*

Even with the best intentions, a playwriting group can become unhelpful to its members, especially if they begin to write to please each other. Some groups dis-solve within six months, while others continue for years. Group support is not automatically good for a playwright, but then neither is constant artistic isola-tion. If you think a playwriting group can help you, find one, or start one. If and when it ceases to be useful to you, move on.

As you work on successive drafts, as you hear them read aloud, you will find yourself dealing with what I call "mathematical" issues. Here are three:

1. *How long should your play be?*

Common wisdom holds that because the attention span of contemporary audiences is limited, plays need to be much more concise, much less discursive, than in earlier times. This is not always true. In a theatrical universe in which Peter Brook's *The Mahabharata,* David Edgar's *Nicholas Nickleby,* and Tony Kushner's *Angels in America* — each of which has more than eight hours of playing time — have been successfully produced worldwide, there are no absolute limits.

Nevertheless, in general, it's more sensible to conform to standard time limits, at least until your name is known well enough to attract an audience for a play of unusual length, or until you are commissioned by a producer to create a work of epic length and scope.

These days, "full-length" plays run from about 90 minutes (without intermission) to 150 minutes in playing time. Your sense of appropriate length can therefore be quite flexible. *Your play should be as long as it takes to present the dramatic experience effectively, and as short as it takes to do so without excess verbiage or imagery.*

2. *How many drafts will you need to do before your script will be finished?*

One draft more than you think.

Each time you finish a draft, you will most likely be convinced that the play is at last done, ready for production. But it may *not* be ready for production; it may not even be ready for submission to theatres.

Each time you finish a draft, put it away and take a break. Come back to it in a few days and reread it aloud to yourself, as you did with your earlier drafts; fix what needs to be fixed, have it read to you by others, then revise it some more.

You may decide to wait until your third or fourth draft is complete before you even ask anyone else to read the roles. That's perfectly reasonable. You may need seven or eight drafts before your play is "ready," whatever that means to you. Again, there are no hard-and-fast rules here, and you will probably misjudge some things on your way to getting them right. Don't panic, don't despair. Keep learning, and keep writing.

In general, you will spend far more time rewriting your script than you spent writing it. The first draft is a valuable asset, but don't confuse the *origin* of a script with its *essence*. That essence may not become clear to you for several drafts' worth of work. You may find the process of revision a rather plodding affair, punctuated by brilliant leaps of insight that can inspire major changes in characters, structure, or tone.

Never forget that you are writing for performance. You don't need to make everything clear on the page; you need to create the verbal and visual cues that trigger a complex, interesting dramatic experience on the stage.

One of the greatest challenges to deal with is time, both within your script and in the outside world. It's hard to be patient when you cannot get the events of your play in the most evocative order, when characters "insist" on remaining elusive, when plots come to a seemingly logical end, then continue on for another scene or two! But patience is exactly what you need. Again, actors may be helpful here. If possible, ask some to work with you on difficult scenes. Together, you may find out how to wind the scene's "inner clock."

Work slowly, carefully, but unselfconsciously.

Find out what questions need to be asked, then pose them clearly to yourself and let your brain function at its own pace. Answers will come, if you do not sabotage the process with too much anxiety or desire to "finish."

3. *"Is your play finished yet?"*

Nothing is more discouraging than well-meaning friends who ask you this question. They often manage to do so just when you are either between drafts or stuck within a draft. Some plays are written quickly, some slowly, and it's impossible to know in advance which will be which. William Saroyan supposedly wrote his play *The Cave Dwellers* from start to finish in just three weeks. Most plays take a good deal longer than that. At the height of his powers, Henrik Ibsen turned out a new play every two years. I've been working on one play for ten years; I wrote another in a month.

Keep to the schedule that you've set for yourself, but detach yourself from calendar time, if you can, while you are writing and rewriting.

How long *does* it take to write a play?

It takes as long as it takes.

One last suggestion about revising your play: Work from the general to the specific. Find the play's major structures of action, get their flow right, and the details will generally fall into place. Sometimes you can work from the specific to the general, and this can be comforting when you are not ready to face major restructuring; but don't get bogged down in trivia.

By the same token, don't cut the little things that give you a unique voice and a point of view unlike anyone else's. Leave some idiosyncrasies.

Above all, in revisions, don't lose the motivation that made you write the play in the first place. Honor that impulse. Keep it alive. And *listen* to the results, all along the way.

❖❖ 10

Getting Your Play Produced

T HERE ARE MANY MORE new plays than there are theatres with production slots available for them, and
regrettably for new playwrights, most new plays never
reach the stage. But many do. How can you see that
your play achieves production?

You've finished your script—or think you have. It's
been through several drafts, perhaps a couple of readings, and the response has been encouraging. Audiences have laughed, misted up, and sucked in their
breath at the right moments, post-reading discussions
have been increasingly positive, and you have done all
the revisions you think the play needs. As far as you can
tell, your play is ready to be considered for production.

Your first goal is to make it stand out in the crowd.
Given the thousands of new plays written every year,
you want yours to look and feel as professional and
worth reading and producing as possible.

So, *presentation* is important.

You may consider this a superficial criterion. But in
the theatre, appearance is reality. It may seem a tri-

umph of form over content for play readers to pay so much attention to the "look" of your script even before they begin to read. However, given the massive workload that most professional readers have, any script that even remotely suggests amateurishness is a likely candidate for the bottom of the "slush pile," where non-priority manuscripts languish and die.

This may seem paradoxical. When your script is one of hundreds, wouldn't you want to draw attention to it by enclosing it in a chartreuse binder, then putting lime-green Day-Glo flowers (with perhaps just a *touch* of glitter) on the title page?

On behalf of all my former scriptreading colleagues, please don't!

Let the quality of the script itself draw attention, not the packaging, no matter how artistic it may be.

Standard formats

In printed playscripts (generally published *after* the play's first production), the standard format requires characters' names in capital letters, set to the left of each speech, like this:

BLANCHE: I have always depended upon the kindness of strangers.

Also, the page is printed on both sides, and there are copious stage directions that describe the setting in minute detail, often indicating specifically where a character is to enter. These directions are frequently accompanied (in the back of the book) by a groundplan from the first production, plus a costume plot, and prop list.

This format provides useful information for subsequent productions of a play, but it is not appropriate for the submission of a new script. If you mimic the published-play format, you will reveal yourself as an amateur.

The playscript that a seasoned playwright submits looks quite different. Character names are usually centered above the line, thus:

BLANCHE
I have always depended upon the kindness of strangers.

The average page of playtext you submit should look something like this:

ALICE
Damn those cops! Your head is still bleeding.

MARTY
Just a scratch. Hey, far out. Really far out, Alice. These dudes on the wall . . . old boyfriends?

ALICE
I wish.

MARTY
Bach, Beethoven, Stravinsky, Mao Tse-tung, Joan of Arc. Now there's a rockin' band.

ALICE
Most people don't recognize more than two of those faces.

MARTY
Most people don't understand political counterpoint.

ALICE
I'm glad you do.

MARTY
It *is* rather droll.

(He touches his wound.)

—Ow!

ALICE

You okay?

MARTY

It stings.

ALICE

Don't touch it. I'll clean it up after the blood clots.

MARTY

Thanks. So. You're a music major?

ALICE

Sociology. Why are cops so violent?

MARTY

Swine flu.

ALICE

I think it's the uniforms. They're hot, and tight, and . . .

MARTY

Minions of capitalism protecting its ill-gotten gains.

ALICE

All you did was burn your draft card.

MARTY

I'm still part of the system. My symbolic action polluted the air.

ALICE

Capitalism makes us all do such horrid things! It's ugly!

MARTY

Yes. But you're beautiful.

ALICE

I am?

MARTY

I think you are. You saved my life back there.

ALICE

Any progressive woman would have. How about some music?

MARTY

Whatcha got?

ALICE

Oh, all kinds. I have . . . Scarlatti. The Rolling Stones. Villa-Lobos. *Annie Get Your Gun.* The Kingston Trio. *Camelot.* Blind Lemon Jefferson. *Missa Luba.*

MARTY

Wow. Eclectic.

ALICE

And Gene Autry singing "Silver Haired Daddy." Anything you want, I can provide.

—from *Mind Over Matter,* my first produced play

In stage directions (always either italicized or underlined), describe the set, and costume and lighting requirements of your play, as minimally as you can. Designers need images that elicit imaginative interpretation, but not a lot of detail. Ideally, you will be part of any pre-production discussions between your director and your designers, at which time the required effect and how best to achieve it will be decided. *Never put your own set or costume designs into the manuscript.*

Indicate at which points in the play characters enter and exit, but do not specify stage right or stage left unless there is a real dramatic need to do so. The cast, together with the director, will make these decisions in rehearsal.

Some anxious beginners add a parenthetical direction to nearly every line, indicating how each is to be spoken; for example:

BLANCHE
(coyly)
I have always depended upon the kindness of strangers.

Finding a parenthetical emotive direction for many lines, as one does in some scripts by new dramatists, is not only annoying, but clear evidence that the playwright is inexperienced in the ways of the theatre. Keep directions on how to say a line to an absolute minimum, and you will stand a far better chance of having actors pay attention to those few that are really necessary. "Necessary" means not obvious from the context. Bear in mind that actors are specialists in the recognition and presentation of emotion. Learn to trust them and their process, which is very different from yours.

Stage directions, which describe action between and during speeches, are usually single-spaced, and set off from the dialogue, as in the above example. It is customary to enclose them in parentheses, but this is less necessary than it was before playwrights could choose italics from their word processor's font library.

The underlying principle is, of course, readability. That is why you should type (or print) on only one side of the page. While this is ecologically wasteful, it is the norm and will likely remain so, in order to facilitate photocopying and faxing of pages.

When theatres ask for scripts to be "securely bound," they do not mean bound like a book. Scripts whose pages cannot be easily photocopied or revised are another mark of the amateur. Rather, pages of your script should have three holes on the left-hand side (leave appropriate margins for this), then secured in a suitable cover. The pages must not be left loose, or your play is doomed (and be sure to number the pages). One quite useful type of cover has a transparent plastic front, so that the title page can be read through it.

Your title page should look like this:

BOX-OFFICE DYNAMITE

a drama in two acts

by

A. Grate Arthur

2468 Easy Street
Cabbageville, NE 12345
(666) 555–1212

© 1999 A. Grate Arthur
All Rights Reserved

Titles

Your play's title is its first interface with the world, so it's important to get it right. Yes, interesting plays with unattractive titles have been produced, but why make it hard on yourself?

Be inspired by the following titles, some of which are better than the plays themselves:

A Streetcar Named Desire
Children of a Lesser God
Like Father, Like Fun
Who's Afraid of Virginia Woolf?

Some plays that have been produced *despite* their titles:

Dusa, Fish, Stas, and Vi
Goebbels' Gobbledegook
Victims Three; or What About Me?

Some plays that have *not* been produced, whose titles may bear some responsibility for that fact:

Flames of Fury
Stupid Boring People and their Horrible Disgusting Lives
The Homosexual Giraffe

No, I'm not making these up! They were actual scripts submitted to various theatres where I have worked.

You may decide on the title of your play before you've written a line of it, or you may go through six drafts and as many titles before you finally settle on a permanent name for your script. Ideally, it will entice an audience at the same time as it conveys to them something important about the play. While an intriguing title is not strictly necessary for production, it may help, and it cannot hurt.

Sometimes, play titles get changed during the rehearsal process, or even between productions. For example, Michael Weller's early play *Cancer* was staged in England before its very successful American premiere under a new—and permanent—title, *Moonchildren*. On the other hand, as the punch line of an old anecdote has it: "Such a lovely play, Mr. Miller, but couldn't you maybe call it *Life of a Salesman?*"

Where (and how) should you submit your script?

Let's assume that you do not yet have an agent to represent you and your scripts to potential producers. Don't worry; an agent is not strictly necessary for you at this point. It's probably better for you to decide how many copies of your script you can afford to send out, and to which theatres. The following advice applies for the most part to not-for-profit resident theatres, since that is where most new plays begin their journeys into the world. But some will be appropriate to commercial producers as well.

If there are any theatres near you that produce (or say they want to produce) new plays, call the theatre and speak with the person who is in charge of reading scripts. His or her title may be artistic director, associate artistic director, artistic associate, dramaturg, or literary manager. Ask what the theatre's current criteria are for considering a new play. Then follow the instructions you are given. These vary widely. You may be asked for a complete copy of the script, a synopsis, or ten to fifteen pages of the text. You may need to include a recommendation from another theatre professional. Be sure to include a cover letter with your submission, whatever form it takes.

Some theatres do not accept "unsolicited" scripts, those that arrive in the mail unannounced. In such a case, write a letter to the artistic director describing your play, and ask if he or she would be interested in reading it. If the answer is yes, your script is no longer unsolicited, and you may indicate "solicited script" on the mailing envelope.

Remember, when you send out a script, to include a manila SASE (self-addressed stamped envelope) for its return. Staple the folded SASE to the inside back cover of your script. If you wish, also include a SASP (self-addressed stamped postcard), requesting that it be mailed to you when the theatre receives your script. You will be expected to pay postage both to and from a theatre that has agreed to read your script; such is the current protocol. You may even be asked to pay a reading fee. I think this is a ripoff, and I would never submit a script to any theatre that requests it. If a theatre wants you to pay them to read your script, ask them if they also charge actors to audition.

When you write a synopsis or description of your play, resist the urge to praise your own work. Maintain a discreet neutrality. List the play's objective requirements, such as the number of male and female characters, settings, and any special needs, such as animals or unusual stage effects. As far as most audiences are concerned, there are only two kinds of play: comedy and drama. Therefore, you should indicate whether your play is, for example, "a comedy in two acts," or "a drama in three acts." If you wish, you may also add a qualifier such as "a tense comedy" or "a political drama," but be careful. Understatement works better.

Now, choosing which theatres to ask to consider your play is not simply a matter of preparing mailing labels for all the producers listed in Theatre Communications Group's annual *Dramatists Sourcebook* or the Dramatists Guild's annual *Resource Directory*. Such a scattershot approach wastes your money, and everybody's time.

Instead, do some research. Decide whether your script is more suitable for summer theatres, which tend to produce lighter fare, than for resident companies with a fall-to-spring season. Find out answers to the following:

- Does this theatre have a history of producing new plays?
- Is your script similar in any way to the new plays that the theatre produces?
- Could your play be an interesting *contrast* to the theatre's typical fare?

These and similar questions will help you narrow your search for a producer to the most likely places.

Send your scripts out, keep good records of where and when you send them, and get on with your next play. Many theatres take several months to respond to a script submission. The reason is simple: Even theatres that specialize in producing brand-new plays do not make reading submitted scripts a priority. Their priority is—as it should be—the production of those plays to which the theatre has already made a commitment. So be prepared to wait, and don't worry.

"Don't worry?" Easy for me to say!

But you've sent your script, you've been waiting for six months, you haven't heard a word, and the theatre claims to respond to submissions within *three* months. Why *shouldn't* you worry?

It's hard to determine from a theatre's silence what that silence means. Has your script been lost in the mail? Possibly. Has it been received, but not yet read? This happens, especially when the reading staff is occupied with other duties (and there are *always* other duties). Has it been read, then passed on to a staff director? If so, that person will read it only when his or her schedule permits. Is the artistic director considering the play for a future season? This part of the wait can be the longest of all.

Some theatres are conscientious about keeping in touch with playwrights as their scripts are being considered, while other theatres are less communicative. Remember, too, that even when your script has been solicited, plays submitted by well-respected agents will be read first, as a professional courtesy.

Give a theatre at least 150% of the time they claim it takes them to read a submission before you call them and ask where your script is in their process. It's not unusual for theatres to receive several hundred new plays each year—some well over a thousand—and many try to give each script two complete readings before returning it or sending it higher in the theatre's chain of decision-making.

Should you submit a play through a director, actor, or member of a theatre's board of trustees?

Most beginning playwrights don't have an "in" like this, and may therefore assume that those who do have an edge. I'm not so sure. But if you know someone who is associated with a theatre, it makes some sense to try this alternate route to production.

Be wary, though. Enterprising playwrights have often attempted to bypass the literary department by handing a script directly to a theatre's artistic director, managing director, or board president. What happens to those scripts? Most get sent right to the literary department for evaluation! You may, however, have saved yourself some waiting time, as these "delegated" scripts tend to have a higher priority than those that simply arrive in the mail.

On the other hand, some scripts that come to a theatre in this way never get read at all. I know at least one artistic director who accepted scripts personally, but never told the literary department about them, and didn't have time to read them himself. Irate playwrights would call asking what had happened to their submissions, only to be told that there was no record that the scripts had ever been received. They had been; they were piling up under the artistic director's bed. This is an extreme case, but such things happen.

What should you do?

It depends. If you know a director whose work you like, contact him or her directly. But be careful, and don't limit your own freedom of choice. I have known theatres to turn down a play that interested them, because they did not admire the talents of the director who brought them the script. The same is true of actors, unless you are dealing with a theatre that has a resident acting company (most do not) and needs to find good roles for them. Even in this case, the dramatic merits of the script itself will have to be strong enough to persuade the theatre's artistic management to take it on.

Sometimes a theatre will be tempted to choose a script just because a popular actor, usually a film or television performer with name recognition and a guaranteed audience, wants to use the play as a star vehicle. There is nothing wrong with this, if the actor is gifted and trained for stage work, but it applies to relatively few new plays. The risk here is that the star's needs may supersede the playwright's, which can really wrench a promising play out of shape.

As for theatre trustees, having one go to bat for your script will probably get it read quickly, just as a courtesy. But even if your script goes straight to the top of the pile, it will still have to impress readers with its quality. The hardest rejection letters to write are those written to VIPs whose play submissions, whether personal or on behalf of others, don't excite a theatre's artistic director enough for him or her to make a commitment. In twenty-some years of work in professional theatre, I have never known a trustee's recommendation of a script to result in a production. But that doesn't mean it hasn't happened, or couldn't happen.

How to deal with rejection letters

Don't take them personally, just keep going.

It is not as easy as many people think to recognize a play's potential merely by reading the script. Theatre history is full of tales about scripts that were rejected by a number of producers, then became big hits when someone saw their possibilities. I know a man who cheerfully admits that he rejected Tom Stoppard's *Rosencrantz and Guildenstern are Dead* on the basis of its title alone. Marsha Norman's *'night, Mother* was called "just another suicide play" by more than one reader. You may get dozens of rejection letters, but it takes *only one* letter of acceptance. So don't give up.

There are three basic types of rejection letters, each of which has many variations. The first—and most common—is the *standard rejection*. Sometimes photocopied, sometimes individualized, this letter will simply return your script and thank you for your interest. No criticism or commentary is offered. You may wonder why the script reader does not tell you what's wrong with your play.

By rejecting your script, the reader is not saying that there is *anything* wrong with it, simply that he or she is not interested in producing the play, or in accepting it into a development program. Don't worry about *why* the theatre isn't interested; there could be many reasons, only a few of which are artistic. Script readers should certainly not offer gratuitous advice on revising the play, unless they mean to make some sort of commitment to it, or to you. Without such a commitment, gratuitous advice is merely patronizing.

Playwrights often wish that they could get more specific reasons for their work's being rejected, but remember that a theatre's primary purpose is to *produce* plays, not to teach people how to write them. However, many theatres that specialize in the production of new plays have strong script development programs, and some of these can be quite helpful. But because these programs do not generate income, their viability depends on a theatre's general financial health and its ability to attract grants for research and development. Therefore, the programs are limited in scope and accept only those few playwrights whose dramatic visions most interest the theatre's artistic team.

The second type of rejection letter will return a submitted script with thanks and a request to see more of your work. Take such a request seriously, because it means that in a sense your next script has already been solicited. Sometimes, such a letter will contain specific suggestions for reworking the play, with a request to submit a revised script. Do so; but be careful. Some theatres ask for revisions without really meaning to suggest a commitment on their part to you or to the script. This seeming thoughtlessness is inadvertent; but if you get such a letter, it is a good idea to contact whoever wrote it and ask them exactly what it means. If you find out, you can decide whether or not to risk a revision "on spec."

The third type of rejection is the rarest, the best, and the most frustrating. It may consist of a letter or a telephone call from the theatre's literary manager or dramaturg, telling you that your play evoked a good deal of excitement, that the theatre is interested in you and your playwriting, but that for some reason they have decided not to take on this particular script. They do, however, want to establish a relationship with you, and they want you to send them any other plays you might have.

What happened? Probably some members of the artistic team at the theatre in question liked your play, while others had reservations. Ultimately it didn't make the cut. But it came close! This is maddening, but it is also good news. Stay in touch with the dramaturg, and learn all you can about the theatre. If it is geographically convenient for you, ask to meet with the artistic director. Find out if the theatre commissions playwrights, or if there is a playwrights' group at the theatre. If you are invited to join a developmental group, or if the theatre offers you a reading, find out specifically what such an offer entails, and good luck.

Agents

What if you get a call offering you a workshop of your play, or even a production?

It's time to get an agent.

I suggested earlier that getting a production should have a higher priority than getting an agent; however, a good agent is a wonderful asset to a playwright. Representation of dramatic authors is a highly specialized profession, and the number of really first-rate play agents is small. As a result, they are besieged by would-be clients, and that is why I would postpone seeking one until you have a production offer in hand.

Then, you can call an agency, explain the situation, and ask them to represent you in contract negotiations on a one-time basis, which can be extended if the working relationship between you and the agency is successful.

Which agency should you call?

You might start with the agent who represents the living playwright whose work you admire most. Published versions of contemporary scripts often indicate who the playwright's agent is; if not, contact the Dramatists Guild in New York City at (212) 398–9366 and ask who represents that author. Then call the agency. If that agent cannot take you on, ask him or her for a referral. Just as a literary manager will read "represented" scripts first, so an agent who knows that a theatre has already picked your play for some level of production will pay attention to this fact.

You may also ask the dramaturg of the theatre that wants to develop or produce your play to recommend a suitable agent for you. The dramaturg might even offer to call an agent on your behalf. Once you have an agent, that person and the theatre's business manager can negotiate an appropriate contract, while you and the artistic staff get on with other important work.

You're on your way.

❖❖ 11

Working with
Dramaturgs
and Directors

C ONGRATULATIONS! Your script has been accepted for
production at a theatre that is well known for its
attention to new playwrights. Now what?

Practical playwriting includes learning how to work
with other artists in the theatre, because your script
cannot truly become a play until it is staged. During
production, you will generally not work directly with
the actors or designers, although you are certainly resources for each other. On artistic matters, you will
communicate primarily through the director. This is as
it should be, because theatrical productions are complex
enough without the immense confusion that results if
lines of communication are not kept simple and clear.
In this protocol, there is room for flexibility, but not
chaos. Therefore, you will probably work most closely
with your dramaturg and your director. They may be
the same person, but more and more frequently, these
two key functions are carried out by different people.

171

Dramaturgs

I've mentioned the word *dramaturg* several times. What, exactly, *is* a dramaturg?

In the American and Canadian theatre, the term (German in origin) refers loosely to a person who advises producers on artistic policy and the selection of plays that best illustrate that policy. Dramaturgs specialize in evaluating and preparing scripts for production, often function as translators or editors of existing plays, and help playwrights and directors develop new texts and productions. Over the last thirty years or so, dramaturgy has become a distinct and recognized profession in North America. Some dramaturgs are permanent staff members of a theatre, some work primarily in universities, while still others are independent artistic consultants hired for individual workshops or productions.

Of course, all dramaturgs are not equally helpful. Be cautious about following the advice you get from anyone until you trust that person's ability to help you realize *your* vision of your play without substituting his or her vision for it. This trust must be earned. Certainly, a talented, trained, experienced dramaturg who understands what you as a playwright are trying to do, who supports and stimulates your particular process with insight and sensitivity, can be a wonderful artistic asset.

Except in unusual circumstances that you decide are appropriate, you should not pay a dramaturg yourself. A dramaturg who is employed by a theatre receives a salary for services rendered. If you have formed a working relationship with a free-lance dramaturg, ask a theatre that makes a financial commitment to you to compensate your dramaturg as well, or to seek support for your artistic team from public or private funding sources. The theatre's fundraising expert (often called "director of development" or some similar title) will be familiar with the standard sources of support for new play development. If you know of another potential source of funds, by all means share this information with the theatre. The development office will be happy to apply for support on your behalf.

A theatre customarily hires free-lance directors and designers, so the principle is well established. Playwrights are generally not hired as short-term employees of a theatre; they are treated, instead, as independent contractors who *license* their plays to the theatre for production. This arrangement keeps copyright and ownership of your play firmly in your hands, where it belongs.

For new plays, there are two kinds of dramaturgy.

The first is *developmental dramaturgy.* During the development of your script from draft to draft, a dramaturg may ask you provocative questions and make pertinent recommendations prior to production that will enable you to make significant improvements to character development, and the progression of scenes.

Here's a recent example of how this works. I served as dramaturg for Todd Hammond's *Starker* for Toronto's Theatre Passe Muraille, which supported a brief workshop of this non-realistic play. With the playwright directing his own work, my task was to help him and the actors agree on the major concerns of the play, then find ways to reveal them more fully in a new draft of the script.

Starker, set somewhere in Europe in the twentieth century, is about a creature—half-man, half-dog—who becomes dictator of a small country at war. Here is the play's first scene in Hammond's second draft:

(Darkness. The sound of bombs exploding in the distance. Lights come up to reveal a large stage curtain, once burgundy and opulent, now stained and torn. Two silent CHORUS MEMBERS, soldiers wearing World War I greatcoats and gas masks, approach the center of the curtain and draw it back to reveal the shattered remains of a library, now used as an operating room. Books and bricks lie scattered about; bandaged SOLDIERS lie groaning on the floor. DOCTORS and NURSES carrying bowls of water and towels scurry around a cloth operating partition. The yelps of a dog giving birth can be heard coming from behind it. Finally, a hairless, naked man, STARKER, slithers off a table behind the partition and onto the floor. A very loud bomb explodes nearby. Two DOCTORS lift STARKER up and carry him downstage as his mother is wheeled offstage. The DOCTORS release him and step back. His legs nearly crumple under the weight, but he finds his balance. His globe-like eyes search for focus. His face turns red and contorts in search of a first rush of air. The DOCTORS frantically motion each other to slap STARKER, but both resist. Then DOCTOR 1 gets an idea. He gingerly approaches STARKER.)

DOCTOR 1
You remember my sister, the concert violinist?

DOCTOR 2
Your what?

DOCTOR 1
My sister the violinist.

DOCTOR 2
You never mentioned—

DOCTOR 1
The young one with such promise, such dreams? My sister?

DOCTOR 2

Umm . . .

DOCTOR 1

Of course you do. Well, while rehearsing with the orchestra—oh, this is so sad . . .

(He begins to cry.)

DOCTOR 2

Sad?

DOCTOR 1

Very.

DOCTOR 2

Oh, sad!

DOCTOR 1

Yes, and, well, while rehearsing with the orchestra,
the tympanist struck his cymbal with such force that it
launched through the air.

DOCTOR 2

Uh huh?

DOCTOR 1

And it swooped down, severing both her hands.

DOCTOR 2

No!

DOCTOR 1

They fell on the floor.

DOCTOR 2

Music was her life.

DOCTOR 1

Now she sits all day and weeps.

DOCTOR 2
Her dreams are dashed.

DOCTOR 1
Tragic, tragic.

(The DOCTORS, NURSES, and wounded SOLDIERS burst into a chorus of weeping. STARKER, however, is quite unaffected, and now blue from lack of air. DOCTOR 1 stops and reconsiders.)

DOCTOR 1
All right then. All right. Um . . . Yes. *(To STARKER, gravely)* You. You are *bad. (Pause.) Very* bad.

DOCTOR 2
Really bad. Shame! Shame on you!

DOCTOR 1
Shame on you!

DOCTOR 2
Bad boy. Really bad. Bad! Bad!

(Pause.)

DOCTOR 1
All right then . . . You . . . you little shit!

DOCTOR 2
Friendless one.

DOCTOR 1
Yes! No friends for you.

DOCTOR 2
No one to love you.

DOCTOR 1
No mother. No father.

DOCTOR 2

All alone. Boo hoo . . .

(STARKER is now green.)

DOCTOR 1

Come on . . . You . . . You will always be alone!

DOCTOR 2

Despised!

DOCTOR 1

Shunned!

DOCTOR 2

Go away.

DOCTOR 1

You're not one of us.

DOCTOR 2

Never will be!

DOCTOR 1

We deny you!

DOCTOR 2

Leave us!

DOCTOR 1

We renounce you!

DOCTOR 2

Leave us!

DOCTOR 1

We've never seen you before!

DOCTOR 2

Leave!

DOCTOR 1

Ignore him, everyone.

DOCTOR 2

He wants to be one of us, but—

BOTH DOCTORS

—He never will be one of us.

(STARKER bursts into hysterical sobs.)

STARKER

Waaahhhh! . . .

(STARKER sucks in a first rush of air, heaving and gasping. His wail echoes throughout the building; tears stream down his face.)

DOCTOR 2

Sorry. We're very sorry.

(DOCTOR 1 motions to two NURSES.)

DOCTOR 1

Wash that muck off him.

(They rush toward STARKER with sponges and buckets of water.)

DOCTOR 1

Quickly, now.

DOCTOR 2

We apologize. That was very cruel of us.

DOCTOR 1
(Examining STARKER)

No paw, no tail, and barely a hair.

DOCTOR 2

And you're *not* not one of us at all.

DOCTOR 1
(in wonder)
A miracle.

DOCTOR 2
We just said that. We lied.

DOCTOR 1
How many fingers do you see?

DOCTOR 2
And we were cruel.

DOCTOR 1
Can. You. Count?

DOCTOR 2
Very cruel. *(Brightly.)* But you're breathing now.

DOCTOR 1
Please count.

DOCTOR 2
That was our intention.

DOCTOR 1
Oh, no. Maybe he can't—

DOCTOR 2
So we're sorry. We're very, very—

(STARKER strains, trying to articulate. With the greatest effort, he forms his lips and slurs:)

STARKER
G . . . g . . .
(Pause.)

DOCTOR 1
What? Oh, my God, did you hear that? Was that a—*(to STARKER)* What was that?

                    STARKER
G . . . g . . . g . . .

                    DOCTOR 2
Oh, my God. Yes! Yes! A consonant. He speaks
consonants.

                    STARKER
l l llooo . . . ooo . . .

                    DOCTOR 1
And yes, Jesus Christ, a vowel!

                    STARKER
R r rr

                    DOCTOR 2
And an R.

                    STARKER
Rreeeeee . . .

                    DOCTOR 1
A definite R.

                    STARKER
Rreeeee . . .

                    DOCTOR 2
Oh, Jesus, such progress.

                    STARKER
Glorrr . . .

                    DOCTOR 2
Miraculous progress.

                    STARKER
Rreee . . .

                    DOCTOR 1
Maybe we're saved.

STARKER

D d da da da dan dan dan youb youb youb youb ube ube übe über über (*Quicker.*) über über über über über *über alles!!*

(Lights out.)

After reading the script, I met with the playwright to discuss his overall intentions, the history of the play (there had been a public reading of the first draft), the conditions of our upcoming workshop, and what he thought needed to be done. I then asked him these questions about Scene 1:

• How will the audience know that the unseen dog's yelps are birthing noises?

• Birth in the midst of wartime carnage—isn't this an unusual activity for battlefield surgeons? Is there something in this fact you can use?

• Why are the doctors reluctant to slap Starker? What would happen if they did so earlier? Is the "no breathing" shtick resonant enough for such an early dramatic image?

• If the doctors' name-calling happened after their standard attempts to get Starker breathing *failed,* what would be the dramatic result?

• Do you run the risk of having an audience blame the doctors for Starker's character because the first words he hears are so dismissive?

• Do you run the risk of having the audience share the doctors' opinion of Starker from the beginning, rather than coming to their own opinions via the action?

• Does verbal abuse make people breathe? Could Starker's inability (refusal?) to breathe be a result rather than a cause?

● Is Starker's first utterance dramatically expansive? Or reductive?

Here is the same scene in the play's third draft, with which we began rehearsals:

(Darkness. The sound of bombs exploding in the distance. Lights come up to reveal a large stage curtain, once burgundy and opulent, now stained and torn. Two silent CHORUS MEMBERS, soldiers wearing World War I greatcoats and gas masks, enter from either side of the stage and slowly approach the center of the curtain. They draw it back to reveal the shattered remains of a library, now transformed into a makeshift operating room. Books and bricks are scattered about; bandaged SOLDIERS lie groaning on the floor. DOCTORS and NURSES scurry around a cloth operating partition with bowls of water and towels. The yelps of a dog giving birth can be heard coming from behind it. Finally, a hairless, naked man, STARKER, slithers off a table behind the partition and onto the floor. A very loud bomb explodes nearby. Two DOCTORS lift up the newborn man, STARKER, and carry him downstage as his mother is wheeled offstage. The DOCTORS release him and step back. His legs nearly crumple under the weight, but he finds his balance. His globe-like eyes search for focus. His face turns red and contorts in search of a first rush of air. The DOCTORS frantically motion each other to slap STARKER's behind, but both resist. Then DOCTOR 1 gets an idea. He gingerly approaches STARKER.)

DOCTOR 1

Oh, I'm so sad!

(He begins to cry, then waves his arms to encourage the others. The whole room—DOCTORS, NURSES, WOUNDED SOLDIERS—bursts into sobs. DOCTOR 1 turns to STARKER.)

DOCTOR 1

Aren't you?

(STARKER is now blue from lack of air. DOCTOR 1 waves off the MOURNERS and reconsiders.)

DOCTOR 1

All right then. Um . . . Yes! *(Gravely)* You. You are bad. *(Slight pause.)* Very bad.

DOCTOR 2

Really bad. Shame! Shame on you!

DOCTOR 1

Double shame!

DOCTOR 2

Bad boy. Really bad.

DOCTOR 1

Bad! Bad!

(STARKER is now green.)

DOCTOR 1

Come on . . . You . . . You will always be alone!

DOCTOR 2

Despised!

DOCTOR 1

Shunned!

DOCTOR 2

Go away.

DOCTOR 1

You're not one of us.

DOCTOR 2

Never will be!

DOCTOR 1

We deny you!

                    DOCTOR 2
Leave us!

                    DOCTOR 1
We renounce you!

                    DOCTOR 2
You don't belong!

                    DOCTOR 1
We've never seen you before!

                    DOCTOR 2
Go!

                    DOCTOR 1
Ignore him, everyone.

                    DOCTOR 2
He wants to be one of us, but—

                 BOTH DOCTORS
—He will never be one of us!

                    STARKER
Waaaaahhhhhh! . . .

(The SPECTATORS cheer.)

                    DOCTOR 1
Sorry! *(He motions to two NURSES.)* Wash that muck
off him.

*(They rush toward STARKER with towels and buckets
of water.)*

                    DOCTOR 1
Quickly, now.

                    DOCTOR 2
Sorry 'bout that.

                    DOCTOR 1
Yes, sorry.

                    DOCTOR 2
That was very cruel of us.

                    DOCTOR 1
And of course you're one of us.

                    DOCTOR 2
We just said that.

                    DOCTOR 1
We're sorry we lied.

                    DOCTOR 2
But we had no other choice.

                    DOCTOR 1
The conditions demanded it.

                    DOCTOR 2
But you're breathing now.

                    DOCTOR 1
Isn't that nice?

                    DOCTOR 2
But we apologize nonetheless.

                    DOCTOR 1
We had no other choice.

                    STARKER
Ggll . . .

                    DOCTOR 1
Oh, my God, he—

(STARKER strains, trying to articulate. With the greatest effort, he forms his lips and slurs:)

                         STARKER
Gggglll . . . lllll . . .

                         DOCTOR 1
Yes. Yes.

                         STARKER
lll . . .

                         DOCTOR 2
A consonant. Oh, a consonant.

                         STARKER
lllooo . . .

                         DOCTOR 1
And a vowel. Yes . . .

                         STARKER
rreeeee oorrr ee. D d da da da dan dan dan youb. Ube
ube übe über über *über alles!!*

(The room cheers. Blackout.)

In his revision, Todd Hammond condensed each *beat*
(unit of action) of the scene, retaining its structure and
arc, but moving it far more quickly to its conclusion.
Then, by having the crowd cheer Starker's outburst,
he effectively made it clear that the whole society was
involved in the creation of the monster we would encounter in later scenes.

If you look closely at Todd's changes to this scene in
light of the dramaturgical questions I asked him, you
will see that there is not a clear relationship between
cause and effect. The playwright did not take my questions as subtle commands, changing his text to answer
directly the concerns that I raised. He could have done
so, for that is always a playwright's option; but the

deeper purpose of my questions was to stimulate Todd's own thinking about his play, not substitute mine for his. At this stage, he chose to condense the play's opening scene, waiting to clarify specific actions until *Starker* is actually "on its feet" preparing to meet an audience. Moreover, since it was clear to both of us that the play needed a good deal more development than it would get during this brief workshop, some of my questions could get short-term answers, while others were meant—and received—as indicators of larger issues, to be dealt with in future pre-production revisions.

As I write this, a Toronto theatre has announced *Starker*'s world premiere, with the playwright directing. Some of my concerns may be dealt with in the staging of the play, while others will be answered (or ignored!) in the written text itself, as it evolves during pre-production, rehearsals, and previews.

The second kind of dramaturgy is *production dramaturgy,* in which a dramaturg asks questions of and gives advice to the *director* in the course of production. As an "objective eye" during rehearsals, the production dramaturg may also continue to work on the text with the playwright and watch the development of the staging to ensure that it continues to express the playwright's intentions and the director's interpretation of them.

Attuned to the intellectual, emotional, social, and symbolic implications of theatre, a good dramaturg can help you see where dramatic problems exist in your script, and can also help the director see where theatrical challenges are likely to occur in the staging. Together, they can then help you decide what strategies of revision will best serve the play's needs in this particular production.

A good dramaturg can help you keep your play's mystery intact by showing you the theatrical effect of dramatic alternatives, then by helping you choose among them. This is what I did for Stephen Reid's play *Doing the Book:* helping the playwright understand where he needed specific, clear dialogue, and where he could rely on actors to get his point across without overemphasizing the obvious.

A good dramaturg will guide you through the often difficult process of translating a play from page to stage. He or she will defend and explain the artistic needs of your script to other theatre practitioners, and can help clarify artistic disagreements so that they do not become personal conflicts.

Ideally, the dramaturg is someone with whom you can discuss not only the particular play you're working on, but plays you have not yet written but merely have a dim notion of. Good dramaturgs can stimulate you to do better work than you thought you could, because they know how playwrights think and how they work.

Most of all, dramaturgs *like* playwrights and celebrate their achievements.

Good dramaturgs will not tell you how to rewrite your play or do it for you; they won't impose their views on your work. They know both dramatic theory and theatre practice, but they will not presume to know how your play *should* be written. They will respect your working process and will support it as much as possible. They should not and usually do not make quick judgments, and they've learned not to offer advice after having read your script—or any revisions—only once.

A conscientious dramaturg will be interested in the theme of your play, and in the issues it addresses. But dramaturgs are less likely to focus on specific issues than on the *hidden* issues, the subtleties and quirks of real dramatic—which is to say human—experience, as reflected in the uniqueness of your characters and action. Good dramaturgs are not dogmatic, except on the issue of quality in theatre. Every good dramaturg is there to support your play and you, in that order. The play comes first.

Directors

Much of what I've said about dramaturgs is true of good directors as well, but there is a crucial difference. The director of your play is responsible for the entire production and must orchestrate the contributions of designers, technicians, production assistants, and—especially—actors. Good directors make this process look smooth and easy, but it isn't.

Once a theatre decides to produce your play, the first question is, "Who will direct it?" You may or may not have much choice in the matter, depending on the level of your experience, but obviously any director selected to stage your play should understand the intent and what elements of it are most important to you. In other words, you and the director need to discuss your script in detail so that you agree artistically.

Directors need to be multitalented, and many are. It's no small achievement to be able to visualize a lengthy crowd scene and then to stage it effectively, focusing an audience's attention on significant details as well as on the whole, without making it obvious to the audience.

Good directors can read a script and see, not just its dramatic potential, but its *theatrical* possibilities, envisioning it in three dimensions, often in a specific playing space. They tend to think concretely and visually about human behavior and are often less interested in themes and symbols than in behavior and timing, in getting a character from the door to the window on *this* line and before *that* line. At the same time, directors must be conscious of a play's *arc of action,* its dramatic superstructure, and most directors will work very hard to keep this arc clear in performance. Above all, directors focus on what is essential for the production. Garland Wright, former artistic director of the Guthrie Theatre in Minneapolis and a sensitive interpreter of plays both old and new, once said, "When I direct a classic play, I'm not interested in what makes it a classic. I'm interested in what makes it a *play.*"

A good stage director must work in both minute detail and large, fluid stage pictures, often simultaneously. He or she must be a visionary, a diplomat, a traffic cop, and sometimes a psychotherapist. Above all, a stage director must be an artist willing to put his or her imagination at the service of the playwright.

Ideally, you, your director, and your dramaturg will explore your script in detail for several hours, over several weeks or months. Designers may also be a part of these discussions. The director may suggest further revisions, and you will have to decide how to respond. Listen closely, ask questions, and try to visualize the suggestions. Don't be defensive, but don't be a doormat. It's still your play, and it always will be.

Casting your play

You will also, ideally, be involved in casting your play. Whether the producing theatre is amateur or professional, this is a fascinating process. You will see a number of different performers attempt to bring to life, on short notice, characters whom you may have taken months or years to create.

Don't expect instant perfection from actors, either in auditions or rehearsals. Inexperienced playwrights are often impatient with the apparent slowness of actors to learn their lines, or to say them confidently or as the playwright intended. Remember, they have spent a lot less time with the characters than you have, and they don't yet know them well, but ultimately, the actors will know your characters better than you do.

Similarly, don't worry if your director spends a lot of time working on *blocking,* which is the technical term for moving actors around the stage. The director, the actors, and even the designers are trying to find the inner life of your play, so that they can merge it with its outer life—the dialogue, the bodies, the sets, costumes, and lights. You can be most helpful by being patient, by taking notes at rehearsals in order to discuss them later with the director and dramaturg, and by learning how other theatre artists work in the extremely short rehearsal time that most plays get in North America.

Your work is far from finished. Moving a script from two dimensions (on paper) to three (on stage) can be exhilarating, but you may find yourself making script revisions right up until opening night. Years ago Moss Hart wrote a very funny play, *Light Up the Sky,* about how this process worked (and didn't work) on Broadway.

Learn how actors, directors, and designers talk to each other. There is a lot of theatre jargon that you will have to master; doing so will increase your credibility with your coworkers. The relationship between playwrights and other theatre people is an odd one; most of your work is done alone and in private, while most of theirs is done collaboratively and in public. But there is genuine respect for what you do. Yes, there are directors who have been heard to mutter, "The only good playwright is a dead playwright," but most theatre people love working on new plays, despite (because of?)

the many unknown and unknowable factors involved in such an adventure.

With your first production, you will have entered a wonderful world that is rarely dull. Once you're part of that world, chances are you'll want to repeat the experience.

This means that you'll have to write another play.

❖ Afterword

W HEN YOU'RE WRITING A PLAY, it's easy to get lost in details, in revisions that seem endless or picayune or both. It's easy to get discouraged, because there are more plays written than produced. You may feel that you are wasting your time by continuing to write them if they are not staged. Even if they *are* staged, audiences may not respond as you would want them to, and critics may do serious damage to your self-esteem.

But playwriting is a profession like no other. It takes guts, and nerve, and ideas, and sheer bloody stubbornness. Talent helps, too, but there are many other attributes necessary for success:

- Passion
- Vision
- Craft
- Intelligence
- Respect for an audience's intelligence
- The ability to be inspired, but not to wait for inspiration
- Willingness to take artistic risks
- Willingness to make mistakes, then repair the damage
- Willingness to learn from anyone and everyone
- Willingness to transform what you learn into art
- Faith in all of the above, and, most of all,
- Faith in yourself.

❖ For Further Reading

Your local library may have many of the plays mentioned in the text. Reading plays is not a substitute for *writing* plays, but it is necessary.

Many of these plays are also available in "acting editions" from either **Samuel French, Inc., 45 W. 25th Street, New York, NY 10010, (212) 206–8990,** or **Dramatists Play Service, Inc., 440 Park Ave. South, New York, NY 10016, (212) 683–8960, www.dramatists.com.**

Where such acting editions exist, they will be noted by (D) for Dramatists, (F) for French.

Albee, Edward. *Who's Afraid of Virginia Woolf?* New York: Atheneum, 1962. (D)

Anderson, Robert. *Tea and Sympathy,* in *Famous American Plays of the 1950's,* New York: Dell, 1988. (F)

Barrie, J.M. *The Old Lady Shows Her Medals,* in Barrie, *Plays,* London: Hodder and Stoughton, 1948. (F)

Beckett, Samuel. *Happy Days,* New York: Grove, 1970. (F)

——————.*Waiting for Godot,* New York: Grove, 1970. (D)

Besier, Rudolf. *The Barretts of Wimpole Street,* Boston: Little, Brown, 1958. (D)

Brecht, Bertolt. *The Caucasian Chalk Circle,* New York: Grove, 1987. (F)

——————.*The Life of Galileo,* London: Methuen, 1987. (F)

——————————. *Mother Courage and her Children,* New York: Grove, 1966. (F)

——————————. *The Resistible Rise of Arturo Ui,* London: Eyre Methuen 1976. (F)

Carrière, Jean-Claude. *The Mahabharata,* New York: Harper & Row, 1987.

Chekhov, Anton. *Ivanov* and *Three Sisters,* both in *Five Plays,* New York: Oxford University Press, 1980. (D)

Churchill, Caryl. *Top Girls,* London: Methuen, 1984. (F)

——————————. *Fen,* in *Softcops and Fen,* London: Methuen, 1986. (F)

——————————. *Cloud 9,* New York: Methuen, 1984. (F)

Dramatists Guild Resource Directory, New York: The Dramatists Guild (annual).

Dramatists Sourcebook, New York: Theatre Communications Group (annual).

Durang, Christopher. *Beyond Therapy,* in *Christopher Durang Explains It All For You,* New York: Grove Weidenfeld, 1990. (F)

——————————. *A History of the American Film,* New York: Avon, 1978. (F)

Edgar, David. *The Life and Adventures of Nicholas Nickleby.* (D)

Eliot, T.S. *Sweeney Agonistes,* in *The Complete Poems and Plays,* New York: Harcourt, Brace & World, Inc., 1962.

Fornés, Maria Irene. *The Conduct of Life,* in *Plays,* New York: PAJ Publications, 1986.

——————————. *A Vietnamese Wedding,* in *Promenade and Other Plays,* New York: PAJ Publications, 1987.

Garcia Lorca, Federico. *Blood Wedding,* in *Three Plays,* New York: Farrar, Straus, Giroux, 1993. (F)

Hart, Moss. *Light Up the Sky.* (D)

Howe, Tina. *The Art of Dining,* in *Three Plays,* New York: Avon, 1984. (F)

Ibsen, Henrik. *Hedda Gabler,* in *Four Major Plays* (tr. Rolf Fjelde), New York: New American Library, 1965. (D), (F)

Jarry, Alfred. *Ubu Roi,* translated as *Ubu Rex* by David Copelin. Vancouver: Pulp Press, 1978. (F)

Jenkin, Len. *Five of Us.* (D)

Kroetz, Franz Xaver. *Request Concert,* in *Farmyard and Four Other Plays,* New York: Urizen, 1976.

Kushner, Tony. *Angels in America, Part One: Millennium Approaches,* New York: Theatre Communications Group, 1993.

——————. *Angels in America, Part Two: Perestroika,* New York: Theatre Communications Group, 1994

——————. *Slavs!,* in *Thinking About the Longstanding Problems of Virtue and Happiness,* New York: Theatre Communications Group, 1995.

Linney, Romulus. *Why the Lord Came to Sand Mountain.* (D)

Ludlam, Charles. *Le Bourgeois Avant-Garde, Camille, The Mystery of Irma Vep, Der Ring Gott Farblonjet,* all in *The Complete Plays of Charles Ludlam,* New York: Harper & Row, 1989. (F)

Mamet, David. *American Buffalo,* New York: Grove Weidenfeld, 1977. (F)

——————. *Edmond,* New York: Grove, 1983. (F)

——————. *Glengarry Glen Ross,* New York: Grove, 1984.(F)

——————. *Sexual Perversity in Chicago,* New York: Grove, 1978. (F)

Mann, Emily. *Execution of Justice,* (F)

——————. *Still Life,* in *Coming to Terms: American Plays and the Vietnam War,* New York: Theatre Communications Group, 1985. (D)

Margulies, Donald. *The Loman Family Picnic,* in *Sight Unseen and Other Plays,* New York, Theatre Communications Group, 1996. (D)

Miller, Arthur. *Death of a Salesman,* New York: Penguin, 1977. (D)

Molière. *The Doctor in Spite of Himself,* New York: Applause Theatre Books, 1987. (F)

——————. *The Middle-Class Aristocrat.* See *The Bourgeois Gentleman,* New York: Applause Theatre Books, 1987. (F)

————————. *Tartuffe,* New York: Harcourt, Brace and World, 1963. (D), (F)

Norman, Marsha. *'night, Mother,* New York: Noonday, 1988. (D)

O'Neill, Eugene. *Long Day's Journey into Night,* New Haven: Yale, 1956. (D)

Pinter, Harold, *Betrayal,* London: Eyre Methuen, 1978. (D)

————————. *The Homecoming,* New York: Grove, 1967. (F)

Rabe, David. *A Question of Mercy,* New York: Grove, 1998. (F)

Saroyan, William. *The Cave Dwellers.* (F)

Shakespeare, William.

Hamlet

Julius Caesar

Macbeth

Richard III

Romeo & Juliet

The Winter's Tale

(All available in numerous editions, such as Penguin)

Shange, Ntozake. *for colored girls who have considered suicide/when the rainbow is enuf,* New York: Macmillan, 1989. (F)

Shaw, George Bernard. *The Dark Lady of the Sonnets* and *Man and Superman,* in *Complete Plays,* New York: Dodd, Mead, 1963. (F)

Shawn, Wallace. *Aunt Dan and Lemon,* New York: Grove, 1985. (D)

Shepard, Sam. *Buried Child* (D), *The Tooth of Crime* (F), and *True West* (F), in *Seven Plays,* New York, Bantam, 1981.

Shue, Larry. *The Foreigner.* (D)

Silver, Nicky. *Fat Men in Skirts, The Food Chain,* and *Free Will and Wanton Lust,* in. *Etiquette and Vitriol: The Food Chain and Other Plays,* New York: Theatre Communications Group, 1995. (D)

Sophocles. *Oedipus Rex,* in *The Complete Plays of Sophocles,* New York: Bantam, 1982.

Stoppard, Tom. *Rosencrantz and Guildenstern are Dead,* New York: Grove Atlantic, 1988. (F)

—————————. *The Real Inspector Hound,* New York: Grove Atlantic, 1970. (F)

—————————. *Travesties,* New York: Grove Atlantic, 1989. (F)

Strindberg, August. *The Father,* in. *Three Plays,* Harmondsworth: Penguin, 1958. (D)

—————————. *The Ghost Sonata,* in *The Chamber Plays,* New York: Dutton,1962 (D)

Synge, J.M. *Riders to the Sea,* London: Methuen, 1961. (F)

Walker, George F.. *Suburban Motel,* Vancouver: Talonbooks, 1997.

Weller, Michael. *Moonchildren,* in *Five Plays,* New York: Theatre Communications Group, 1998. (F)

Wilde, Oscar. *The Importance of Being Earnest,* London: Eyre Methuen, 1966. (F)

Williams, Tennessee. *Cat on a Hot Tin Roof,* New York: New Directions, 1975. (D)

—————————. *The Glass Menagerie,* New York: Random House, 1945. (D)

—————————. *A Streetcar Named Desire,* New York: New Directions, 1980. (D)

Wilson, August. *Fences,* New York: New American Library, 1986. (F)

—————————. *The Piano Lesson,* New York: Dutton, 1990. (F)

—————————. *Seven Guitars,* New York: Dutton, 1996. (F)

❖ Index

❖ About the Author

DAVID COPELIN is a playwright, dramaturg, essayist, and translator. Educated at Columbia University and the Sorbonne, he received a Doctor of Fine Arts degree in Criticism and Dramatic Literature from Yale University. Mr. Copelin has worked as literary manager and/or dramaturg for the Mark Taper Forum, New Dramatists, the Phoenix Theatre, Arena Stage, Actors Theatre of Louisville, Magic Theatre, PlayLabs, and Marin Theatre Company in the United States, and for Theatre Passe Muraille and Cahoots Theatre Projects in Canada.

He has also been a consultant for the National Endowment for the Arts, Theatre Communications Group, the Rockefeller Foundation, the California Arts Council, the Austin Arts Commission, the United States Information Agency, and the Berkeley Community Fund. He has taught theatre at San José State University, the University of California (Davis and San Diego), New York University, Louisiana State University, St. Edward's University, and the University of Texas at Austin, and has published articles in *Theatre Journal, The Drama Review, Theater,* and *The Writer.*

Mr. Copelin has also served as story advisor for Warner Bros., CBS Theatrical Films, and CBS/Fox Video, as well as Associate Producer of the PBS series "Made in America." His adaptation of Alfred Jarry's *Ubu Roi* has been widely produced in North America. A member of the Dramatists Guild and of the Playwrights Union of Canada, he was a founding member of Literary Managers and Dramaturgs of Americas, serving a term as its President.

He now lives in Toronto, where he writes plays, is a freelance dramaturg, and serves as Administrator of the Institute for Family Living. He is married to psychotherapist Diane Marshall.